CAMBRIDGE
UNIVERSITY PRESS

CAMBRIDGE
Primary Mathematics

Learner's Book 6

Mary Wood, Emma Low, Greg Byrd & Lynn Byrd

CAMBRIDGE
UNIVERSITY PRESS

University Printing House, Cambridge CB2 8BS, United Kingdom

One Liberty Plaza, 20th Floor, New York, NY 10006, USA

477 Williamstown Road, Port Melbourne, VIC 3207, Australia

314–321, 3rd Floor, Plot 3, Splendor Forum, Jasola District Centre, New Delhi – 110025, India

103 Penang Road, #05–06/07, Visioncrest Commercial, Singapore 238467

Cambridge University Press is part of the University of Cambridge.

It furthers the University's mission by disseminating knowledge in the pursuit of education, learning and research at the highest international levels of excellence.

www.cambridge.org
Information on this title: www.cambridge.org/9781108746328

First published 2014
Second edition 2021

20 19 18 17 16 15 14 13 12 11 10 9 8

Printed in Malaysia by Vivar Printing

A catalogue record for this publication is available from the British Library

ISBN 978-1-108-74632-8 Paperback with Digital Access (1 Year)
ISBN 978-1-108-96421-0 Digital Learner's Book (1 Year)
ISBN 978-1-108-96420-3 Learner's Book eBook

Additional resources for this publication at www.cambridge.org/go

Projects and their accompanying teacher guidance have been written by the NRICH Team. NRICH is an innovative collaboration between the Faculties of Mathematics and Education at the University of Cambridge, which focuses on problem solving and on creating opportunities for students to learn mathematics through exploration and discussion: nrich.maths.org.

Introduction

Welcome to Stage 6 of Cambridge Primary Mathematics. We hope this book will show you how interesting Mathematics can be and make you want to explore and investigate mathematical ideas.

Mathematics is everywhere. Developing our skills in mathematics makes us better problem-solvers through understanding how to reason, analyse and reflect. We use mathematics to understand money and complete practical tasks like cooking and decorating. It helps us to make good decisions in everyday life.

In this book you will work like a mathematician to find the answers to questions like these:

- What is the value of $2 + 2^2 + 2^3$?
- Which would you choose 20% of \$10 or $\frac{1}{10}$ of \$20?
- What is a common multiple?
- Why is the answer to $3 \times (4 + 5)$ different to the answer to $3 \times 4 + 5$?
- What time is it in Mumbai when it is 9 a.m. in Mexico City?
- What is a reflex angle?
- How do you draw a waffle diagram?
- How can a shape be translated?

Talk about the mathematics as you explore and learn. This helps you to reflect on what you did and refine the mathematical ideas to develop a more effective approach or solution.

You will be able to practise new skills, check how you are doing and also challenge yourself to find out more. You will be able to make connections between what seem to be different areas of mathematics.

We hope you enjoy thinking and working like a mathematician.

Mary Wood, Emma Low, Greg Byrd and Lynn Byrd

Contents

How to use this book

In this book you will find lots of different features to help your learning.

Questions to find out what you know already. ⟶

Getting started

1   What is the value of the digit 9 in these numbers?

   a   809.46   b   2021.89   c   123 456.95

2   Write these numbers in words and digits.

   a   200 000 + 5000 + 400 + 8 + 0.9

   b   500 000 + 70 000 + 30 + 6 + 0.01

3   a   What number is ten times bigger than 0.01?

   b   What number is one hundred times smaller than 555?

4   What is the missing number?

   $100 \times 10 = 10\,000 \div \boxed{}$

What you will learn in the unit. ⟶

We are going to ...

- explain the value of each digit in numbers with up to 3 decimal places
- multiply and divide whole numbers and decimals by 10, 100 and 1000
- compose, decompose and regroup numbers with up to 3 decimal places.

Important words that you will use. ⟶

bisect   decompose

diagonal   justify

parallel   trapezia

Step-by-step examples showing a way to solve a problem. ⟶

Worked example 1

Write this as a decimal number.

$3 + \frac{6}{1000} + 10 + \frac{3}{100} + \frac{1}{10}$

$10 + 3 + \frac{1}{10} + \frac{3}{100} + \frac{6}{1000}$

Write the terms in order of size, starting with the one with the highest place value.

Put the digits in a place value grid.

10	1	•	$\frac{1}{10}$	$\frac{1}{100}$	$\frac{1}{1000}$
1	3	•	1	3	6

Answer: 13.136

There are often many different ways to solve a problem.

These questions will help you develop your skills of thinking and working mathematically.

> 3 Find the odd one out.
>
> 1.234   1234 thousandths   12.34
>
> 123.4 hundredths   123 hundredths and 4 thousandths
>
> Explain your answer.

An investigation to carry out with a partner or in groups.
Where this icon appears ◀○, the activity will help develop your skills of thinking and working mathematically.

Think like a mathematician

Daphne the dog had four litters of puppies. The mean average number of puppies in a litter was 5. Investigate how many puppies could be in each litter. Find different ways that make the mean average 5.

What do you notice about the total number of puppies in each solution where the mean is 5?

Check that it is true for another solution. Explain what you find out.

Questions to help you think about how you learn.

Think about your answer. Are there any other possible answers? How do you know? Did you think about checking your answer with your partner?

What you have learned in the unit.

Look what I can do!

- ☐ I can explain the value of each digit in numbers with up to 3 decimal places.
- ☐ I can multiply and divide whole numbers and decimals by 10, 100 and 1000.
- ☐ I can compose, decompose and regroup numbers with up to 3 decimal places.

Questions that cover what you have learned in the unit.

Check your progress

1 Hassan counts in steps of 0.4.

His first number is 1.

He counts 1, 1.4, 1.8, ...

What is the tenth number in his sequence?

 ❯ Project 4

At the end of several units, there is a project for you to carry out using what you have learned. You might make something or solve a problem.

Projects and their accompanying teacher guidance have been written by the NRICH Team. NRICH is an innovative collaboration between the Faculties of Mathematics and Education at the University of Cambridge, which focuses on problem solving and on creating opportunities for students to learn mathematics through exploration and discussion: nrich.maths.org.

Ordering times

Put these lengths of time in order, from shortest to longest.
You might like to use a calculator to help you.

A second	Time since you were born	A thousand seconds	A decade
Time for light to reach the Earth from the Sun	A minute	Time it takes you to eat a meal	100 000 hours
1000 months	A century	A day	Time it takes you to say the alphabet
A month	1000 days	Time since the last Olympic Games	A fortnight
Time it takes the Moon to go once around the Earth	A year	5 000 000 minutes	Time since the invention of the telephone

Thinking and Working Mathematically

There are some important skills that you will develop as you learn mathematics.

Specialising
is when I choose an example and check to see if it satisfies or does not satisfy specific mathematical criteria.

Characterising
is when I identify and describe the mathematical properties of an object.

Generalising
is when I recognise an underlying pattern by identifying many examples that satisfy the same mathematical criteria.

Classifying
is when I organise objects into groups according to their mathematical properties.

Critiquing
is when I compare and evaluate mathematical ideas, representations or solutions to identify advantages and disadvantages.

Improving
is when I refine mathematical ideas or representations to develop a more effective approach or solution.

Conjecturing is when I form mathematical questions or ideas.

Convincing
is when I present evidence to justify or challenge a mathematical idea or solution.

1 The number system

1 What is the value of the digit 9 in these numbers?

   a 809.46   b 2021.89   c 123 456.95

2 Write these numbers in words and digits.

   a $200\,000 + 5000 + 400 + 8 + 0.9$

   b $500\,000 + 70\,000 + 30 + 6 + 0.01$

3 a What number is ten times bigger than 0.01?

   b What number is one hundred times smaller than 555?

4 What is the missing number?

   $100 \times 10 = 10\,000 \div$ ☐

5 Round these lengths to the nearest whole number.

   a 6.2 m   b 36.5 cm   c 12.3 m   d 10.6 cm

6 A number with 1 decimal place is rounded to the nearest whole number.

   a What is the smallest number that rounds to 100?

   b What is the largest number that rounds to 10?

Numbers are important. We use them every day.

- We use a series of digits when we telephone a friend.

- We use decimal numbers when we work out prices.

- We use positive and negative numbers when we use a thermometer.

When do you use numbers? Make a list.

Here are some ideas to help you get started.

> 1.1 Place value

We are going to ...

- explain the value of each digit in numbers with up to 3 decimal places
- multiply and divide whole numbers and decimals by 10, 100 and 1000
- compose, decompose and regroup numbers with up to 3 decimal places.

You already know how to read and write decimal numbers with 1 or 2 decimal places.

You can compose, decompose and regroup numbers, and you can multiply and divide by 10, 100 and 1000.

The Western Pygmy Blue Butterfly is very small. Some have a wingspan of only 0.375 inches, which is between 9 and 10 millimetres.

> compose numbers   decimal point
> decompose   digit
> hundredth   place value
> regroup   tenth   thousandth

In this unit, you will learn about numbers with 3 decimal places.

Worked example 1

Write this as a decimal number.

$3 + \dfrac{6}{1000} + 10 + \dfrac{3}{100} + \dfrac{1}{10}$

$10 + 3 + \dfrac{1}{10} + \dfrac{3}{100} + \dfrac{6}{1000}$

Write the terms in order of size, starting with the one with the highest place value.

Put the digits in a place value grid.

tenths
hundredths
thousandths

10	1	$\frac{1}{10}$	$\frac{1}{100}$	$\frac{1}{1000}$
1	3	1	3	6

Answer: 13.136

Exercise 1.1

1   What is the value of the digit 7 in these numbers?

   a   6703.46   b   213.807   c   456.702   d   60.078

2   Sonia has these five cards.

   What is the smallest number, greater than 1, she can make using all her cards?

 3   Find the odd one out.

   1.234   1234 thousandths   12.34

   123.4 hundredths   123 hundredths and 4 thousandths

   Explain your answer.

4 Add these numbers together and write the total number in words and digits.

    a   2 + 0.1 + 0.03 + 0.009

    b   –900 – 9 – 0.9 – 0.009

    c   20 + 5 + 0.4 + 0.03 + 0.001

    d   –3 – 0.4 – 0.08 – 0.001

Swap books with your partner and check their answer.
Read the numbers to each other.

5 Copy and complete.

$$37.844 = 30 + 7 + \boxed{} + 0.04 + \boxed{}$$

6 Petra is regrouping decimal numbers.

She spills ink on her work.

What number is under each ink blot?

    a $0.546 = 0.4 + \blacksquare + 0.006$

    b $0.789 = 0.7 + 0.07 + \blacksquare$

7 Find the missing numbers.

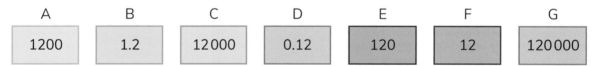

    a $7.2 \times 1000 = \boxed{}$

    b $0.85 \times 100 = \boxed{}$

    c $4.28 \times 10 = \boxed{}$

    d $670 \div 100 = \boxed{}$

    e $151 \div 1000 = \boxed{}$

    f $5.5 \div 10 = \boxed{}$

Check your answers with your partner.

8 Look at these number cards.

A	B	C	D	E	F	G
1200	1.2	12 000	0.12	120	12	120 000

Write the letter of the card that is:

    a   one thousand times bigger than 12

    b   one hundredth of 12

    c   one thousandth of 120 000.

9 Mira divides a number by 10, then by 10 again and then by 10 again.

Her answer is 0.005.

What number did she start with?

Did you find any question particularly hard? Why?
If you are asked to do similar questions, what would
you do differently?

Think like a mathematician

There are 10 trees in the Numberland Woods.

Each tree has 10 branches. Each branch has 10 twigs.
Each twig has 10 flowers. Each flower has 10 petals.

Sofia went into the woods.

She took 1 petal, 1 flower, 1 twig and 1 branch.

How many petals are left in the woods?

Look what I can do!

☐ I can explain the value of each digit in numbers with up to 3 decimal places.

☐ I can multiply and divide whole numbers and decimals by 10, 100 and 1000.

☐ I can compose, decompose and regroup numbers with up to 3 decimal places.

> 1.2 Rounding decimal numbers

We are going to ...

- round a number with 2 decimal places to the nearest whole number
- round a number with 2 decimal places to the nearest tenth.

Rounding makes it easier to describe and understand numbers. It is easier to understand that Usain Bolt ran 100 metres in less than 10 seconds than he ran 100 metres in 9.63 seconds.

nearest

round

Worked example 2

Round these numbers to the nearest tenth.

a 8.80   b 6.45   c 3.95

a 8.8	b 6.5	c 4.0	If the hundredths digit is 0, 1, 2, 3 or 4, round down by keeping the tenths digit the same.
			If the hundredths digit is 5, 6, 7, 8 or 9, round up by increasing the value of the tenths digit by 1. If the tenths digit is 9, it will change to 0 and the ones digit will increase by 1.
			There must always be 1 decimal place in the answer, even if it is zero.

Exercise 1.2

1   Round these decimals to the nearest whole number.

   4.09   **7.89**   **2.55**   7.45

2   Leo bought a book costing $14.65.

   What is the cost of the book to the nearest dollar?

3   Which of these numbers rounds to 5 when rounded to the nearest whole number?

    4.35   4.05   4.5   5.05   4.55   5.35   5.5   5.53

Check your answers to questions **1** to **3** with your partner.

4   Round these numbers to the nearest tenth.

    4.52   7.81   2.35   9.07

5   Which of these numbers rounds to 7.5 when rounded to the nearest tenth?

    7.35   7.05   7.51   7.55   7.49   7.56   7.53

Check your answers to questions **4** and **5** with your partner.

 6   Correct all the statements that are false.

    A   3.04 is 3 when rounded to the nearest whole number and the nearest tenth.

    B   5.03 is 5 when rounded to the nearest whole number and 5.0 when rounded to the nearest tenth.

    C   6.95 is 7 when rounded to the nearest whole number and 6.9 when rounded to the nearest tenth.

    Discuss your answers with your partner.
    Make sure you explain the reasons you have given.

7   Round these measures to the nearest tenth.

    55.55 litres   12.22 metres   35.45 kilograms

8   Choose the **smallest** number from this list that rounds to 1.

    0.55   0.99   1.9   1.45   0.5   1.05   0

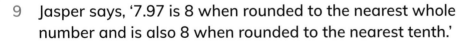 9   Jasper says, '7.97 is 8 when rounded to the nearest whole number and is also 8 when rounded to the nearest tenth.'

    Is Jasper correct?

    Explain your answer.

Look back over your answers.
Did you use the worked example to guide you?
Did you find any question particularly hard? Why?

Think like a mathematician

The sides of a rectangular face on a cuboid are measured in centimetres to 2 decimal places using a micrometer (an instrument for measuring length accurately).

The measurements are rounded to the nearest whole number. They are 5 cm and 6 cm.

What is the smallest possible perimeter of the rectangle?

What is the largest possible perimeter of the rectangle?

Investigate the smallest and largest perimeters for other rectangles if the measurements have been rounded to the nearest centimetre.

You will show you are **specialising** when you work out solutions.

If you explain your results for a number of rectangles, you will show you are **convincing**.

Tip

Think about the smallest number with 2 decimal places that rounds to 5 cm, then think about the largest number with 2 decimal places that rounds to 5 cm. Do the same for 6 cm.

Look what I can do!

- ☐ I can round a number with 2 decimal places to the nearest whole number.
- ☐ I can round a number with 2 decimal places to the nearest tenth.

Check your progress

1   Copy and complete.

$87.655 = 80 + 7 + \boxed{} + \boxed{} + \boxed{}$

2   What decimal number is represented by the following?

$90 + 7 + \dfrac{3}{10} + \dfrac{1}{100} + \dfrac{4}{1000}$

3   How many times bigger is the value of the digit 6 in 64.53 than the value of the digit 6 in 0.367?

4   a   What is 3.08 rounded to the nearest tenth?

   b   What is 9.55 rounded to the nearest whole number?

5   Find the missing numbers.

   a $\boxed{} \times 0.9 = 9$ b $705 \div \boxed{} = 7.05$

   c $\boxed{} \times 0.16 = 160$ d $34 \div 1000 = \boxed{}$

6   The announcer said, 'Ingrid won the 100 metre race in 13.9 seconds.'

Her time was originally measured to 2 decimal places.

What was the slowest time she could have run?

2 ▶ Numbers and sequences

1   These patterns of dots show the first three square numbers.

Write the first ten square numbers.

2   Given the first term and the term-to-term rule, write down the first six terms of each sequence.

a   First term: 4, term-to-term rule: add 7

b   First term: 2, term-to-term rule: add 9

3   The numbers in this sequence increase by equal amounts each time.

What are the three missing numbers?

1, ☐ , ☐ , ☐ , 13

4   Here is a set of numbers.

2   4   6   12   24   36   48

a   Choose three multiples of 12 from the set.

b   Choose three factors of 12 from the set.

Look at these sequences.

Can you think of other examples of sequences?

In this unit you will explore sequences of numbers and different types of numbers including square and cube numbers, common multiples and common factors.

› 2.1 Counting and sequences

We are going to ...

- count on and back using fractions and decimals
- find and use the position-to-term rule of a sequence.

In Stage 5, you learned how to use a term-to-term rule to find the next term in a sequence. In this unit, you will learn how to use the position-to-term rule to find *any* term in a sequence.

position-to-term rule

term

term-to-term rule

Position	Term
1	4
2	8
3	12
4	16

+4
+4
+4

Multiply by 4

The 25th term is 25 × 4 = 100.

Worked example 1

a   Follow the instructions in the flow diagram to generate a sequence.

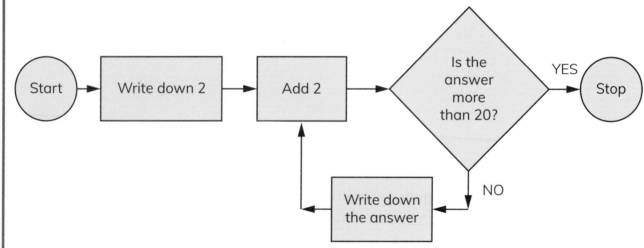

Continued

b   What is the position-to-term rule for the sequence?

c   Imagine the sequence continues forever.
    What is the 50th term in the sequence?

---

a   2, 4, 6, 8, 10, 12, 14, 16, 18, 20   Follow the instructions in the flow diagram.

We include 20 because it is not 'more than 20'.

b

Position	Term
1	2
2	4
3	6

Make a table to show the position and the term.

Look at how the position number is connected to the term number.

⟶

Multiply by 2

The position-to-term rule is: multiply by 2.

Use the position-to-term rule to find the 50th term.

c   50 × 2 = 100

Exercise 2.1

1   a   Find the position-to-term rule for the numbers in this table.

Position	Term
1	6
2	12
3	18
4	24
10	

b   What is the 10th term of the sequence 6, 12, 18, ...?

2   The numbers in this sequence increase by equal amounts each time.

a   Write the three missing numbers.

3, ☐ , ☐ , ☐ , 15

b   What is the term-to-term rule for the sequence?

c   What is the position-to-term rule for the sequence?

3   a   Follow the instructions in the flow diagram to generate a sequence.

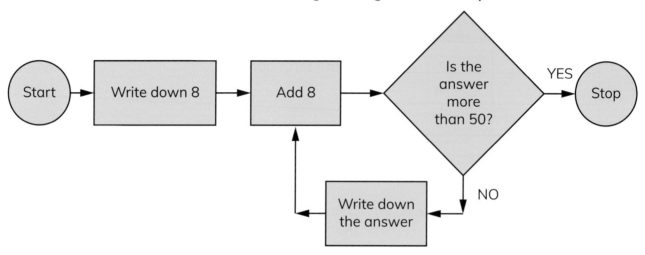

b   What is the position-to-term rule for the sequence?

c   Imagine the sequence continues forever.
    What is the 50th term in the sequence?

4   Here is the start of a sequence of shapes using rectangles and triangles.
    Each rectangle is numbered.

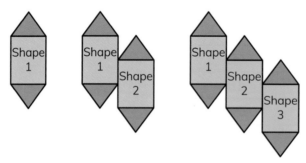

The sequence continues in the same way.

a   How many triangles are there in the shape with 50 rectangles?
    How many rectangles and triangles are there altogether in that shape?

b   Jodi starts to make a table showing the position (shape number) and the term (total number of rectangles and triangles). Copy and complete her table.

Position	Term
1	3
2	
	9
	12
5	

c   What is the position-to-term rule for Jodi's sequence?

d   What is the 20th term in the sequence?

Check your answers with your partner.

5   Pablo counts on in quarters.

What are the two missing numbers?

$\frac{1}{4}$ $\frac{1}{2}$ $\frac{3}{4}$ 1 $1\frac{1}{2}$ 2

6   a   Write a sequence with steps of constant size in which the first term is 1 and the fifth term is 1.04.

b   What is the 10th term?

> **Tip**
>
> Beware! The answer is not 1.1.

 7   Ollie writes a number sequence starting at 15 and counting back in steps of 0.4.

15, 14.6, 14.2, 13.8, …

He says, '−1.5 cannot be in my sequence.'

Ollie is correct. How do you know without counting back?

Discuss your answer with your partner.

8   Hassan counts back in steps of $\frac{2}{5}$ starting at 0.

He counts 0, $-\frac{2}{5}$, $-\frac{4}{5}$, $-1\frac{1}{5}$, …

Which of these numbers should Hassan say?

$-1\frac{4}{5}$ -2 -3 $-3\frac{3}{5}$ -4

25 ⟩

9 Samira counts on from 20 in steps of 1.001

20   21.001   22.002   23.003 ...

Write the first number Samira says which is bigger than 30.

Think back over the work you have done on sequences.
What have you learned?
Is there anything you need to get better at?

Think like a mathematician

The diagram shows the first five hexagonal numbers:
1, 6, 15, 28, 45, ...

3rd hexagonal number: 15
2nd hexagonal number: 6
1st hexagonal number: 1

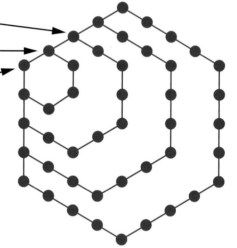

How does the sequence continue? What is the next number in the sequence?

Write these numbers as the sum of two hexagonal numbers: 12, 21, 29, 30.

The first one is done for you.

12 = 6 + 6

Investigate which other numbers, less than 100, can be written as the sum of two hexagonal numbers.

Count the dots inside and on the perimeter of each hexagon

You will show you are **specialising** when you investigate which other numbers, less than 100, can be written as the sum of two hexagonal numbers.

Look what I can do!

☐   I can count on and back using fractions and decimals.

☐   I can find and use the position-to-term rule in a sequence.

⟩ 2.2 Special numbers

We are going to ...

- work out the square number in any position, for example, the ninth square number is $9 \times 9 = 81$
- use the notation ^{2} to represent squared
- know the cube of numbers up to 5, for example, $5^3 = 5 \times 5 \times 5$ or $5^2 \times 5$ which is 125.

Have you ever tried to solve the Rubik's cube puzzle?

cube number

square number

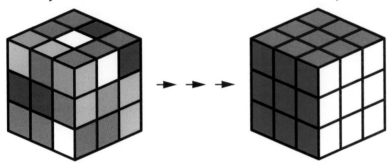

How many small cubes make up the large cube?

In this section you will learn about cube numbers. A square number is a number you get when you multiply an integer by itself. A cube number is a number you get when you multiply an integer by itself and by itself again. 2^2 means 2 squared, which equals the square number 4. 2^3 means 2 cubed, which equals the cube number 8.

Worked example 2

Which is larger?

2^3 or 3^2

Explain your answer.

Answer: $3^2 > 2^3$	Explain your answer by showing the calculations for
$2^3 = 2 \times 2 \times 2 = 8$	2^3 and 3^2.
$3^2 = 3 \times 3 = 9$	$9 > 8$

Exercise 2.2

1   What is the ninth square number?

2   Calculate.

   a 5^2 b 10^2 c 7^2

3   Find two square numbers that total 45 when added together.

4   Here are three cubes of increasing size.

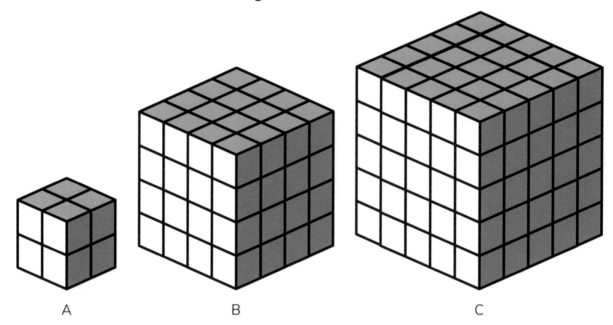

A   B   C

How many small cubes are in each of the large cubes?

> **Tip**
>
> In cube A: There are 2 small cubes along each edge
>   There are 4 or 2^2 small cubes in each layer
>   There are 8 or $2^2 \times 2$ or 2^3 small cubes in cube A

5   Calculate.

   a 5^3 b 1^3 c 3^3

Check your answers to questions **4** and **5** with your partner.

6   Copy this Carroll diagram and write a number less than 100 in each section.

	Odd	Not odd
Cube number		
Not a cube number		

7   Find two cube numbers that total 152 when added together.

8   Classify these expressions into two groups. Explain how you chose the groups.

2^3 3^2 $2^3 + 1$ half of 4^2 $3^2 - 1$ $2^2 \times 2$

Discuss your answer with your partner.

Think like a mathematician

Adding two consecutive square numbers

1 and 4 are two consecutive square numbers. 1 + 4 = 5

4 and 9 are two consecutive square numbers. 4 + 9 = 13

Investigate the sums of two consecutive square numbers.
If you are systematic you should find an interesting pattern.

Adding odd numbers

The first two odd numbers are 1 and 3. Their sum is 4.

The first five odd numbers are 1, 3, 5, 7 and 9. What is their sum?

Investigate the sums of consecutive odd numbers starting at 1.
What do you notice?

You will show you are **conjecturing** if you set yourself questions to
answer as you investigate the numbers.

You will show you are **convincing** when you explain your results.

Look what I can do!

☐   I can work out the square number in any position, for example,
the ninth square number is $9 \times 9 = 81$.

☐   I can use the notation ^{2} to represent squared.

☐   I can work out the cube of numbers up to 5, for example, $5^3 = 5 \times 5 \times 5$ or $5^2 \times 5$
which is 125.

> 2.3 Common multiples and factors

We are going to ...

- find common multiples
- find common factors.

Imagine you have this bar of chocolate. You divide it between you and your friends so you all have the same number of pieces.

common factor

common multiple

factor   multiple

You can divide it equally between 2 people, 3 people, 4 people, 6 people, 8 people, 12 people or 24 people.

We say that 24 is a common multiple of 2, 3, 4, 6, 8, 12 and 24.

In this section you will learn about common multiples and common factors.

Worked example 3

Anna is thinking of a number.

She says, 'My number is a multiple of 3 and 5 and is less than 20.'

What number is Anna thinking of?

Multiples of 3 are:	The answer must be less than 20.
3, 6, 9, 12, 15, 18	

Continued

Multiples of 5 are:

5, 10, 15

You need to find a **common multiple** of 3 and 5, so the answer must appear in both lists.

Answer:

Anna is thinking of 15.

Exercise 2.3

1   Write the numbers in the correct place on a copy of the Venn diagram.

5   14   15   18   20   21   24   29   **30**   60

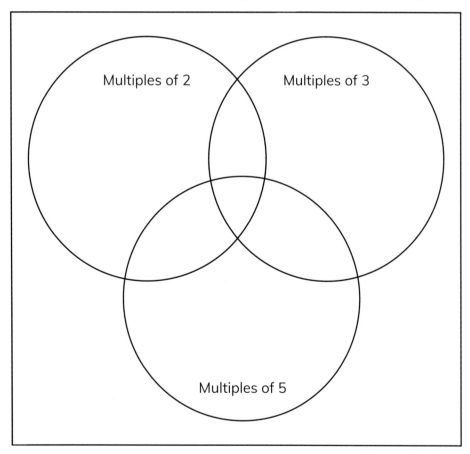

Which numbers are common multiples of 2, 3 and 5?

Discuss your answer with your partner. Do you agree with each other?

2   The numbers in this sequence increase by 3 each time.

3, 6, 9, 12, ...

The numbers in this sequence increase by 5 each time.

5, 10, 15, 20, ...

Both sequences continue.

Write a number bigger than 100 which is in **both** sequences.

3   Write all the common multiples of 3 and 8 that are less than 50.

4   Olivia and Amir play football regularly.

Olivia plays once every 4 days.

Amir plays once every 3 days.

If they both play football today, how many times in the next fortnight will they play on the same day?

Are you using common multiples or common factors in your answer? Explain the difference.

5   a   Write the factors of 18.

b   Write the factors of 24.

c   Draw a ring around the common factors.

6   Write all the factors of 30 that are also factors of 20.

 7   Pierre gives 32 football cards to his friends.

He shares them equally so all his friends have the same amount.

How many friends could Pierre have? Explain your answer.

Think about your answer. Are there any other possible answers? How do you know? Did you think about checking your answer with your partner?

8   Isabella has three digit cards.

[1]   [5]   [6]

Which two cards could she use to make:

a   a common multiple of 5 and 13?

b   a common factor of 60 and 90?

Think like a mathematician

The sequence 4, 2, 1, 3 uses the numbers 1 to 4 so that each number is either a factor or a multiple of the previous number.

Each number is used once only.

Find a similar sequence that uses the numbers 1 to 6.

Tip

Use digit cards that you can easily move around.

You will show you are **specialising** when you find solutions to the problem.

Look what I can do!

☐   I can find common multiples.

☐   I can find common factors.

Check your progress

1 Hassan counts in steps of 0.4.

His first number is 1.

He counts 1, 1.4, 1.8, ...

What is the tenth number in his sequence?

2 a Find the position-to-term rule for the numbers in this table.

Position	Term
1	7
2	14
3	21
4	28

b What is the 10th term of the sequence 7, 14, 21, ...?

3 Which of these expressions are equal to 7^2?

7×7 $7 + 7$ $2 \times 2 \times 2 \times 2 \times 2 \times 2 \times 2$

$7 + 7 + 7 + 7 + 7 + 7 + 7$ 7×2

4 Mia is thinking of a number.

She says, 'My number is an even number less than 50. It is a common multiple of 3 and 7.'

What number is Mia thinking of?

5 Tim goes to school.

His age is a cube number.

His age is double one square number and half a different square number.

How old is Tim?

> Project 1

Odd sequence

Zara and Arun's teacher wrote this on the board:

1, 4, 9, ...

What do you notice?

Talk to a partner about what you both noticed.

They are square numbers.

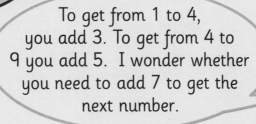

To get from 1 to 4, you add 3. To get from 4 to 9 you add 5. I wonder whether you need to add 7 to get the next number.

Do you agree with Zara's observation? Do you agree with Arun's? Why or why not?

Continue the sequence to find the next three terms.

Will the number 63 be part of the sequence? How do you know? Try to answer without continuing the sequence any further.

Why does adding consecutive odd numbers produce square numbers?

You might like to explain in words, through pictures, or using both.

3 ▶ Averages

1   What colour flower is the mode in each picture?

a

b

c

Continued

2   Some children have been put into groups.
    What is the median age of each group?

<u>Group A</u>   <u>Group B</u>

5 years old   8 years old

6 years old   4 years old

7 years old   7 years old

<u>Group C</u>   <u>Group D</u>

11 years old   12 years old

9 years old   10 years old

6 years old   12 years old

10 years old   11 years old

7 years old   9 years old

3   A shop sells tops in sizes 1, 2, 3, 4 and 5.

These are the sizes that were sold this week.

5, 2, 4, 2, 3, 2, 1, 2, 5, 4, 5

The shopkeeper wants to work out the average size sold so that he knows which top to stock more of in the shop.

Should the shopkeeper use the median or mode average?

Why?

You can use averages to help you understand data in real life.
Averages can tell you things like the most common score or height.
Averages can tell you about the most popular flavour or music group.

In this unit you will learn more about three types of average called the **mode**, **median** and **mean**. You will also learn about what the **range** of a set of data can tell us.

These are the throws of two javelin throwers.

Which javelin thrower do you think is the best and why?

| 1.6 m | 1.8 m | 2.0 m | 2.2 m | 2.4 m | 2.6 m | 2.8 m |

The averages and range can help us describe and compare sets of data. Knowing the averages and range would help us to argue which of the javelin throwers is the best.

> 3.1 Mode, median, mean and range

We are going to ...

- find the mode and median of sets of data
- find the mean and range of sets of data
- use the average and range to describe sets of data and answer questions.

Averages can help you solve problems and make decisions. When people review a book out of 10 all their reviews are put together and the average number is found. Look at these book review scores:

average	bimodal
mean	median
mode	range

Average
6 out of 10

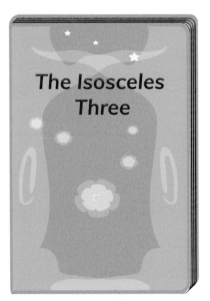

Average
7 out of 10

How do you think the averages were worked out?

Is it possible that nobody scored *The Midnight Story* 6 out of 10?

Is it possible that someone scored *The Isosceles Three* 0 out of 10?

The average represents what a typical person might think about the book. How can you use the average score to help you decide if you want to read one of the books?

> **Worked example 1**
>
> Hari wants to find out if he is tall for his age.
>
> He measures the heights of 6 children that are the same age as him. He chooses to calculate the mean of the heights to find the average height of the children so that he can compare his height to the average height.
>
> What is the mean of these heights?
>
> 138 cm, 140 cm, 136 cm, 141 cm, 142 cm, 137 cm
>
> | | |
> |---|---|
> | 138 + 140 + 136 + 141 + 142 + 137 = 834 | Add all the heights together. |
> | | You can use mental or written methods, or use a calculator as appropriate. |
> | There are 6 heights in the set of data. | Count how many heights there are in the set of data. |
> | 834 ÷ 6 = 139 | Divide the total of all the heights by the number of heights in the set of data. |
> | The mean of the heights is 139 cm. | Make sure you write your answer using the correct units. |

Exercise 3.1

1   Write the modes and median of each set of measures.

   a   4 cm, 4 cm, 5 cm, 5 cm, 6 cm, 7 cm

   b   51 mm, 47 mm, 51 mm, 53 mm, 59 mm, 59 mm

   c   1.2 m, 1.8 m, 1.1 m, 2.1 m, 1.2 m, 1.8 m, 1.6 m, 1.4 m

   d   101 cm, 106 cm, 95 cm, 105 cm, 102 cm, 102 cm, 97 cm, 101 cm

> **Tip**
>
> Sometimes a set of data has more than one mode. If the data has two values that both occur the most often then it is 'bimodal' and both of the numbers are the mode.

2   What is the mean for each set of numbers?

   a   5, 6, 7   b   9, 9, 2, 8   c   10, 12   d   2, 3, 4, 5, 6

> **Tip**
>
> Remember to put the numbers in order to find the median.
> Sometimes the middle of the pieces of data does not land on a value.
>
> $$\downarrow$$
> $$1 \quad 4 \quad 5 \quad 7 \quad 8 \quad 8$$
>
> Imagine the data were on a number line. The number that is halfway between
> the two pieces of data in the middle is the median. (If you are not sure, add the
> two pieces of data in the middle together then divide by 2.)
>
> $$6$$
> $$\downarrow$$
> $$1 \quad 4 \quad 5 \quad 7 \quad 8 \quad 8$$

3   a   Which of these bowlers has the
       highest mean bowling score after
       six games?

> **Tip**
>
> You could use a
> calculator or computer
> to add and divide
> the numbers.

	Game					
	1	2	3	4	5	6
Player A	95	108	99	120	95	101
Player B	109	130	124	111	145	131
Player C	138	130	151	157	153	165
Player D	98	154	160	91	129	118

   b   Players B and D both have the same mean bowling score.
       Which do you think is the better player? Write a sentence to
       convince your partner that B or D is better. Use information from
       the table in your sentence.

4   Sarah and Anita both practise playing the guitar for 5 days.

This table shows how long each child practised for on each of the 5 days.

	Day 1	Day 2	Day 3	Day 4	Day 5
Sarah	10 minutes	8 minutes	2 minutes	10 minutes	20 minutes
Anita	10 minutes	8 minutes	12 minutes	10 minutes	10 minutes

Each child has practised for 50 minutes in total.

Copy and complete these sentences using the information in the table.

The range of Sarah's practice times is

_____ minutes.

> **Tip**
>
> To find the range, subtract the lowest value from the highest value.

The range of Anita's practice times is _____ minutes.

_____ has the smallest range of times, so she is more consistent in the amount of time she practises for over the 5 days.

5   Find the range of each set of numbers.

a   1, 2, 3, 4   b   7, 7, 12, 2

c   34, 33, 70, 5, 6, 8   d   26, 21, 35, 63, 30

e   11, 10, 15, 13, 11   f   25, 34, 28, 29

g   91, 105, 116

6   Find the range in heights of these two groups of children.

Group 1		Group 2	
127 cm	130 cm	137 cm	131 cm
152 cm	138 cm	129 cm	143 cm
135 cm	138 cm	136 cm	143 cm
141 cm		132 cm	

Which group has the largest range?

Describe how the two groups would look different because of their different ranges.

7   Kali, Summer, Benji and Kyle are learning to skip.

While they were practising they recorded how many skips they
did in a row.

Here are their attempts:

	1st try	2nd try	3rd try	4th try	5th try	6th try	7th try
Kali	6	5	6	6	8	11	7
Summer	3	0	3	8	0	7	0
Benji	0	0	1	0	4	0	2
Kyle	4	7	7	6	2	5	4

a   Copy and complete this table:

	Range	Mode	Median	Mean
Kali				
Summer				
Benji				
Kyle				

b   Who do you think has been most successful at skipping?
Explain your answer using the information in your table.

c   Which average do you think is most appropriate for describing the average
number of skips a child has done? Why?

Reflect on how well you are remembering which measure
is which and the words mode, median, mean and range.
Do you have a good strategy for remembering?
If not, ask someone else about their strategy.

8 Gabriella and Demi have recorded the temperature in the shade at midday on every day of their six week school holiday.

	Sunday	Monday	Tuesday	Wednesday	Thursday	Friday	Saturday
Week 1	25 °C	20 °C	20 °C	19 °C	20 °C	24 °C	26 °C
Week 2	25 °C	25 °C	28 °C	27 °C	28 °C	31 °C	25 °C
Week 3	28 °C	27 °C	27 °C	27 °C	24 °C	22 °C	20 °C
Week 4	15 °C	19 °C	23 °C	19 °C	16 °C	15 °C	19 °C
Week 5	18 °C	19 °C	20 °C	23 °C	25 °C	28 °C	28 °C
Week 6	33 °C	34 °C	32 °C	26 °C	26 °C	29 °C	30 °C

a Design a table to record the three types of average and the range for each week of the holiday. Complete your table with the averages and range.

b Which week had the greatest range of temperatures?

c Use the information in your table to argue which was the warmest week of the holiday.

d Gabriella and Demi were taking part in a conservation project on every Tuesday of the holiday. What was the range of temperatures on Tuesdays? What was the average (mode, median and mean) temperature on Tuesdays?

9   The four fictional countries of Fratania, Spanila, Brimland and Gretilli
    celebrate a dry weather festival during the months of January
    to May. They are each trying to encourage tourists to visit their
    own countries. Here are graphs of each country's rainfall last year
    for the five months of the festival.

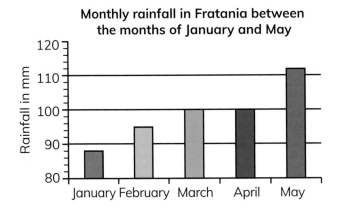

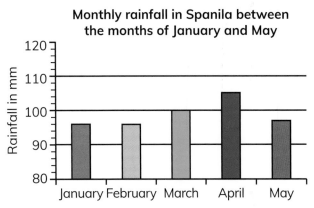

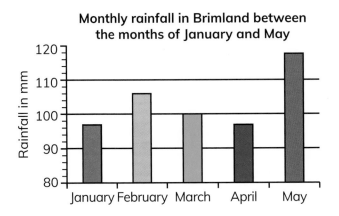

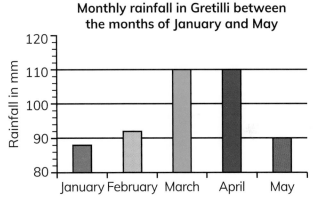

Which average (mode, median or mean) would be best for each
country to advertise the lowest possible average rainfall for the season?

Think like a mathematician

Daphne the dog had four litters of puppies. The mean number
of puppies in a litter was 5. Investigate how many puppies could be
in each litter. Find different ways that make the mean 5.

What do you notice about the total number of puppies in each solution
where the mean is 5?

Specialise by checking that it is true for another solution.

Generalise by explaining what you find out.

Look what I can do!

☐ I can find the mode and median of sets of data.

☐ I can find the mean and range of sets of data.

☐ I can use the average and range to describe sets of data and answer questions.

Check your progress

1 Write the mode, median, mean and range for each set of numbers.

a 4, 7, 5, 4, 10

b 7, 3, 13, 1, 7, 5

c 21, 29, 31, 40, 29, 30

d 6, 9, 12, 15, 11, 14, 11, 6

2 Seven buckets were put out to collect money for a charity.

The amounts on the buckets show how much was collected in that bucket.

$34 $0 $42 $51

$0 $263 $37

Work out the mode, median and mean of the amounts collected.

Which best describes the average amount of money collected? Why?

› Project 2

Sneaky statistics

The children in Sofia's class are collecting stickers that are sold in packs at their local shop.

Every Friday, Sofia's dad gives her enough money to buy two packs of stickers. Sofia decides to collect some information about how many stickers her friends are buying and compare that to how many she buys each week.

Sofia asks ten friends how many packs of stickers they bought last week. They tell her the following numbers:

1, 1, 1, 1, 2, 2, 2, 3, 3, 14

What do you notice about these numbers?

Can you think of a reason why one child might have bought 14 packs of stickers last week?

Sofia asks her dad if he can give her enough money to buy three packs of stickers this week.

On average, each of my friends bought three packs of stickers last week!

Which average is Sofia using here? Why has she chosen to use that average?

If Sofia's dad looks at the same data, what could he say in response?

Which average do you think is the most helpful here? Why?

Continued

In Marcus's class, the children are collecting stickers that can be bought individually.

Marcus asks ten friends how many stickers they bought last week. He finds that there is only one mode, which is four stickers. The median is four stickers as well, and the mean is also exactly four stickers.

> Think about some different possible numbers of stickers that each of the ten people might have bought.
>
> What is the smallest possible range that this data could have?
>
> If the range was 15, how many stickers would each of the ten people have bought? Could the range be larger than 15? Why or why not?

Getting started

1 Each shape stands for a number.
   Find the value of each shape.

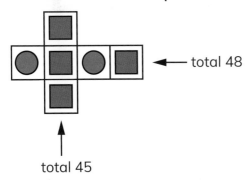

◀— total 48

↑
total 45

2 The table shows the number of people who choose running,
   swimming and cycling on 3 days at an activity centre.

	Monday	Tuesday	Wednesday
Running	2134	1121	3154
Swimming	2168	2142	2138
Cycling	3214	1198	1131

   a How many people go cycling on Monday and Tuesday?

   b How many more people go running on Wednesday than go
      swimming on Wednesday?

3 Calculate.

   a −7 + 2   b 4 − 8   c −1 + 2

Every year the number of animals at the zoo is recorded.
It takes about a week to count all the different kinds of animals.

The board shows the number of penguins in the zoo.

PENGUINS

MALE: 35

FEMALE: 38

JUVENILES: 22

What is the total number of penguins?

What is the difference between the number of adults and the number of juveniles?

To answer these questions you need to add and subtract.

This unit is all about adding and subtracting whole numbers.
Later in this book you will add and subtract fractions and decimals.

› 4.1 Positive and negative integers

We are going to ...

- estimate, add and subtract large integers
- add and subtract positive and negative integers
- find the difference between two integers.

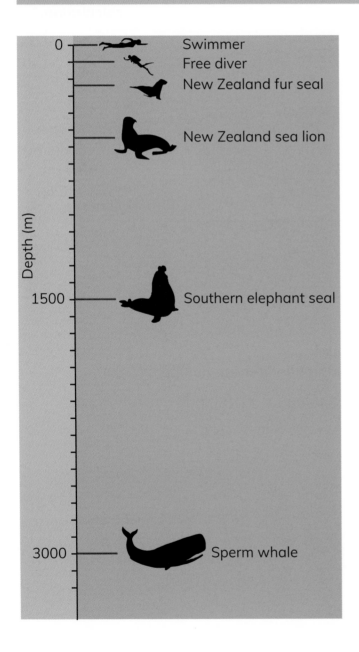

This diagram shows the maximum known diving depths for human and other marine mammals.

How much deeper can the sperm whale dive compared to the elephant seal?

> integer
> negative number
> positive number

Worked example 1

The temperature outside is −30 °C.

a   The temperature rises by 5 °C. What is the new temperature?

b   The original temperature falls by 5 °C. What is the new temperature?

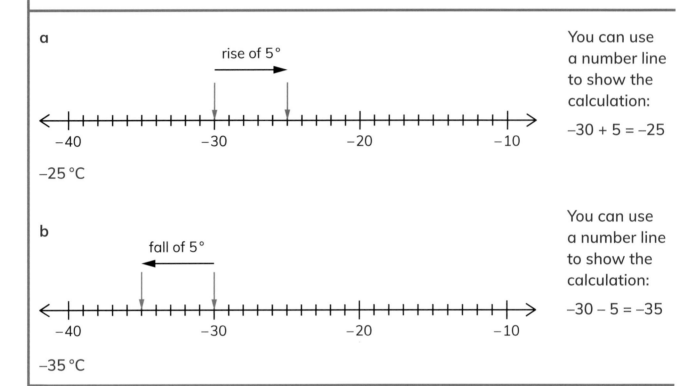

a

rise of 5°

−25 °C

You can use
a number line
to show the
calculation:

−30 + 5 = −25

b

fall of 5°

−35 °C

You can use
a number line
to show the
calculation:

−30 − 5 = −35

Exercise 4.1

1   Estimate the answer to each calculation using one of these numbers.

110 000   120 000   130 000   140 000   150 000

a   34 405 + 90 253 =

b   278 410 − 139 321 =

2   The table shows the flight distance from Dubai to five destinations.

Destination	Distance in kilometres
Buenos Aires	13 656
Cairo	2419
Karachi	1190
New York	11 020
Singapore	5847

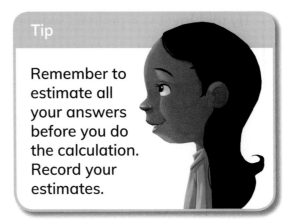

Tip

Remember to estimate all your answers before you do the calculation. Record your estimates.

a   Liu flies from Dubai to Singapore. Nadine flies from Dubai to Cairo. What is the difference in their flight distances?

b   Mary lives in Dubai. In one year she travels to Buenos Aires, Cairo and Karachi. She returns home after each trip. How many kilometres does she fly altogether?

Check your answers using a calculator.

3   Ravi completes a subtraction calculation, but his answer is wrong.

$$
\begin{array}{r}
3\ 6\ 8\ 0\ 4 \\
-\quad 5\ 7\ 2\ 4 \\
\hline
3\ 1\ 1\ 8\ 0 \\
\hline
\end{array}
$$

Write an explanation to convince Ravi that he is wrong.
Correct his answer.

4   Faizah plays a game. She has 5398 points.

She scores another 465 points.

Her target is 6000 points.

How many more points does she need to reach her target?

5   Here is part of a temperature scale showing the temperature at Coldpark.

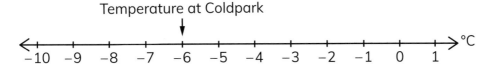

Temperature at Coldpark

The temperature falls by 3 °C. What is the new temperature?

6 The temperature at 8 a.m. is –1 °C.

   By midday it is 4 degrees warmer. What is the temperature at midday?

7 The maximum temperature in Mongolia during October is 15 °C.

   This temperature decreases by 12 °C each month from October to February.

   What is the maximum temperature in January?

   Check your answer with your partner. Do you agree?

8 The thermometers show the temperatures in Ulaanbaatar and
   Montreal on the same day.

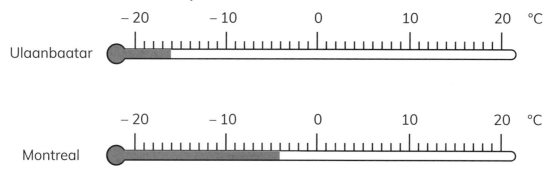

   What is the difference in temperature between
   Ulaanbaatar and Montreal?

9 Here is a table of temperatures in five cities
   during one morning.

   Tip

   Remember that
   a difference is
   always positive.

City	Temperature
London	4 °C
Moscow	–10 °C
Oslo	–5 °C
Tokyo	2 °C
Ulaanbaatar	–29 °C

   a What is the difference in temperature between London and Oslo?

   b What is the difference in temperature between Moscow
      and Ulaanbaatar?

   c What is the difference in temperature between the warmest city
      and the coldest city?

10 Find the difference between each pair of numbers.

a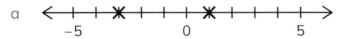

b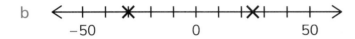

Number lines can help with calculations. Sometimes one is shown in the question, but sometimes you need to draw your own. Look at the questions in this exercise and think about how you have used number lines to help you.

Think like a mathematician

	Example
Choose three digits.	
Arrange them in order, biggest first. This is your first three-digit number.	7 2 4
Reverse the order of the digits. This is your second three-digit number.	7 4 2
Find the difference between the two three-digit numbers.	2 4 7
	742 − 247 = 495
Reverse the order of the digits in the answer.	594
Add these final two three-digit numbers together.	495 + 594 = 1089

Do this several times with different digits. What do you notice?

Start with four digits. What do you notice?

Predict what the answer will be if you start with two digits. Test your prediction. Was your prediction correct?

You will show you are **generalising** when you notice something about your results.

You will show you are **conjecturing** when you predict what will happen with two digits.

Tip

Always record a 2 digit-number when you find the difference. For example, the difference between 76 and 67 is 09.

Look what I can do!

☐ I can estimate, add and subtract large numbers.

☐ I can add and subtract positive and negative numbers.

☐ I can find the difference between two numbers.

› 4.2 Using letters to represent numbers

We are going to ...

- find the value of a letter that represents a number
- use the idea that an unknown is not necessarily one fixed number but a variable.

Look at this shape puzzle. Each shape represents a number. The numbers the shapes represent are added. What number does each shape stand for?

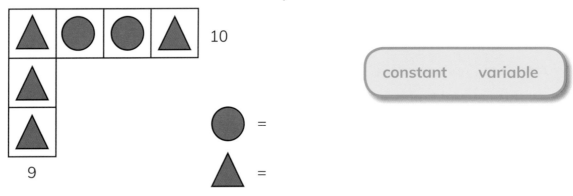

constant   variable

In this unit, you will use a letter to stand for a value as in these examples.
What are the values of a and b?

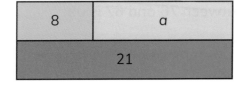

a =   b =

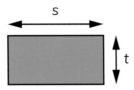

Worked example 2

The perimeter of this rectangle is 20 cm.

s and t represent the lengths of the sides of the rectangle.

What are the possible values of sides s and t?

s = 1 cm and t = 9 cm	The sum of the lengths of the sides is equal to 20 cm.
s = 2 cm and t = 8 cm	
s = 3 cm and t = 7 cm	
s = 4 cm and t = 6 cm	s + t is half the distance round the rectangle so s + t = 10.
s = 5 cm and t = 5 cm	
s = 6 cm and t = 4 cm	
s = 7 cm and t = 3 cm	
s = 8 cm and t = 2 cm	
s = 9 cm and t = 1 cm	

Exercise 4.2

1   Cheng plays a board game using a dice.

He uses the instructions together with his dice score to work out how many spaces he moves.

d represents the dice score.

For example:

Score	Calculate	Spaces moved
	$d + 4$	9 spaces

Work out how many spaces Cheng moves.

	Score	Calculate	Spaces moved
a		$d - 3$	
b		$6 - d$	
c		$4 + d$	

2   For each pair of expressions write 'equal' or 'not equal'.

a $d + 4$ $4 + d$

b $2 + d$ $d + 2$

c $5 - d$ $d - 5$

3   Khalid says, '$d + 3$ is the same as $3 + d$ so $d - 3$ must be the same as $3 - d$.' Is Khalid correct? Explain your answer.

4 Martha buys 2 more pairs of socks than shoes.

a Copy and complete the table where x represents the number of pairs of shoes and y represents the number of pairs of socks.

x	1	2	
y	3		6

b Write a number sentence linking x, y and 2.

5 This puzzle has 9 pieces.

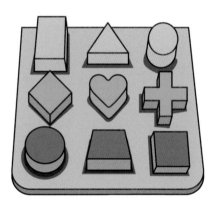

Hassan places 1 or more shapes and Sanjay places the other shapes.

a Copy and complete this table to show the number of pieces each person places.

x (number of pieces placed by Hassan)									
y (number of pieces placed by Sanjay)									

b Write a number sentence linking x, y and 9.

6   a and b represent the lengths, in centimetres, of two strips of card.
b is 3 cm longer than a.

The two strips are placed end to end.

The total length is 15 cm.

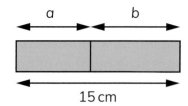

Find the values of a and b.

7   The perimeter (p) of a square is the sum of the lengths of the sides.

s represents the length, in centimetres, of a side.

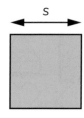

$$p = s + s + s + s$$

a   What is the value of p when s = 5?

b   What is the value of p when s = 7?

c   What is the value of s when p = 32?

8   This isosceles triangle has a perimeter of 15 cm.

x and y represent the lengths, in centimetres, of the sides of the
triangle shown in the diagram.

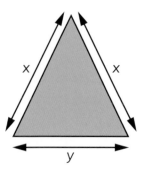

a   Find three possible sets of values for x and y.

b   Write a formula for the perimeter (p) of the triangle using x and y.

How do questions **7** and **8** compare with questions you answered on perimeter when working on measures?
Look out for links within mathematics and in other subjects where you use mathematics.

Think like a mathematician

a, b and c each represent a whole number from 1 upwards.

$$a + b + c = 7$$

Find all the possible values for a, b and c.
How many different solutions can you find?

You will show you are **specialising** when you find all the possible values for a, b and c.

Check your answers with your partner.
How did you make sure you had found all the solutions?

Look what I can do!

☐ I can find the value of a letter that represents a number.

☐ I can use the idea that an unknown is not necessarily one fixed number but a variable.

Check your progress

1 Copy and complete this calculation.

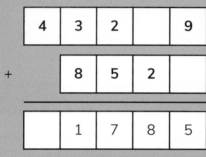

4	3	2		9

+		8	5	2	

		1	7	8	5

2 The table shows the temperatures in six cities on the same day in January.

City	Temperature
Buenos Aires	29 °C
Tallinn	−1 °C
Abu Dhabi	18 °C
Moscow	−10 °C
Oslo	−5 °C
Vancouver	7 °C

   a The temperature in Moscow rises by 5 °C. What is the new temperature?

   b What is the difference between the temperatures in Tallinn and Moscow?

3 The diagram shows three strips placed end to end. m and n represent the lengths, in centimetres, of strips of card. The total length is 17 cm.

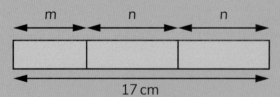

17 cm

> **Tip**
>
> Remember that the diagram shows
> $m + n + n = 17$.
> Compare this number sentence with
> $m + n = 10$ to find the value of n.

Lisa knows that $m + n = 10$

Show how she can find the value of m and n.

5 ▶ 2D shapes

Getting started

1   Match each shape **A** to **F** with its correct name card **i** to **vi**.
    The first one is done for you: **A** and **iii**.

A    B    C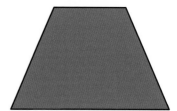

D    E    F

i | rectangle   ii | kite   iii | parallelogram

iv | trapezium   v | square   vi | rhombus

2   Write down the number of lines of symmetry for each of these triangles.

a   isosceles triangle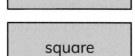

b   scalene triangle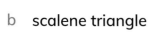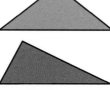

c   equilateral triangle

Continued

3 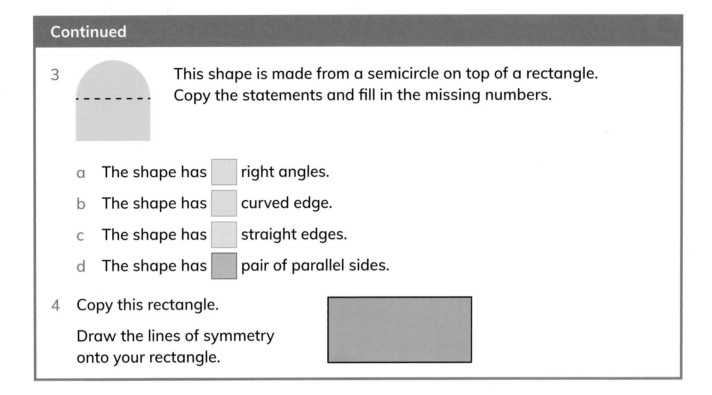 This shape is made from a semicircle on top of a rectangle. Copy the statements and fill in the missing numbers.

a The shape has ☐ right angles.

b The shape has ☐ curved edge.

c The shape has ☐ straight edges.

d The shape has ☐ pair of parallel sides.

4 Copy this rectangle.

Draw the lines of symmetry onto your rectangle.

Shapes and symmetry play an important part in our everyday lives. When you go into a grocery store and look at the food on the shelves, what shapes can you see?

Graphic designers are people who decide what shape boxes, tins or packets are going to be used for different foods. They also design the patterns and writing on the boxes, tins or packets. They want to make them look as good as possible so that you will want to buy them!

> 5.1 Quadrilaterals

We are going to ...

- identify quadrilaterals
- describe quadrilaterals
- classify quadrilaterals
- sketch quadrilaterals.

Quadrilateral tiles are often used on kitchen and bathroom walls and floors. This is because they fit together exactly leaving no spaces (tessellate). You need to be able to identify and describe the different types of quadrilaterals. This is really important when you need to order tiles for your house.

bisect	decompose
diagonal	justify
parallel	trapezia

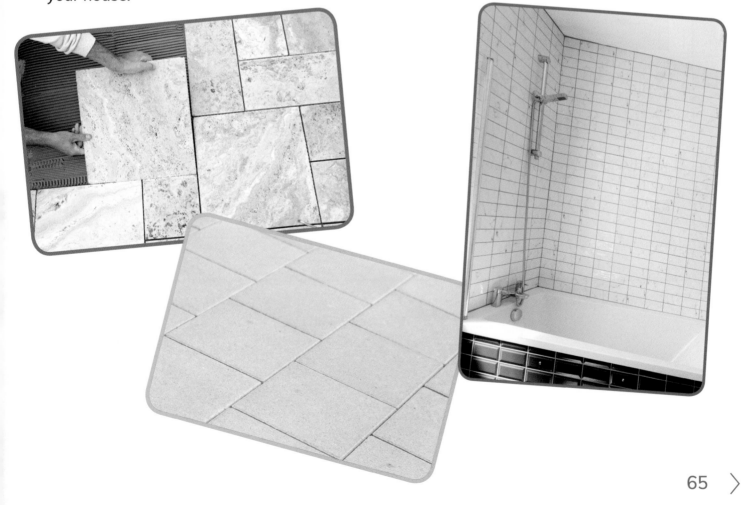

Worked example 1

Describe the characteristics of a rectangle. Show each one on a diagram.

A rectangle is a quadrilateral.

This is the same as saying it has four sides.

It has two pairs of equal sides.

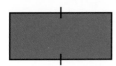

The symbol | shows one pair of equal sides and the symbol = shows the other.

It has two pairs of parallel sides.

The symbol ∧ shows one pair of parallel sides and the symbol >> shows the other.

The sides meet at 90°.

The square symbol ⌐ shows that two sides meet at 90°.

The diagonals bisect each other.

The diagonals cut each other exactly in half.

It has two lines of symmetry.

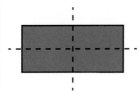

It has a horizontal _ _ _ and a vertical ⋮ line of symmetry.

Exercise 5.1

 1 Copy and complete these characteristics of a square. Show each one on a diagram. Diagrams **a**, **b** and **e** have been done for you.

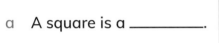

a A square is a _____.

b It has _____ equal sides.

c It has _____ pairs of parallel sides.

d The sides meet at _____°.

e The diagonals _____ each other at 90°.

f It has _____ lines of symmetry.

 2 Copy and complete these characteristics of a parallelogram. Show each one on a diagram. Diagrams **a**, **d** and **f** have been done for you.

a A parallelogram is a _____.

b It has _____ pairs of equal sides.

c It has _____ pairs of parallel sides.

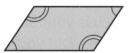

d It has _____ pairs of equal angles.

Tip

The single curved lines show that these two angles are equal.

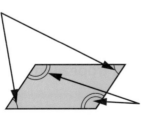

The double curved lines show that these two angles are equal.

e   The diagonals _____ each other.

f   It has _____ lines of symmetry.

Think like a mathematician 1

Work with a partner to answer these questions.

The diagrams **A** to **F** show different **trapezia**.

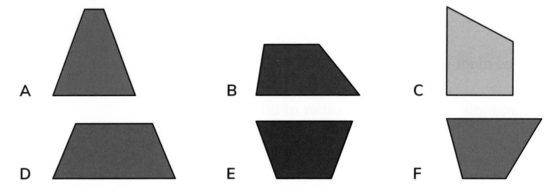

A   B   C

D   E   F

a   Classify these trapezia by sorting them into two groups.
Group 1: trapezia that are isosceles
Group 2: trapezia that are not isosceles

b   Write down the properties of

   i   an isosceles trapezium.

   ii   a trapezium that is not isosceles.

   Show each property on a diagram.

> **Tip**
>
> 'Properties' is a word that is often used instead of 'characteristics'.

c   Compare and discuss your answers to parts **a** and **b** with other learners in your class. Did you write down all the properties? If you did not, write them down now so that you do not forget them.

> **Tip**
>
> Where have you met the word isosceles before?
> What do you think is special about an isosceles trapezium?

3 a Make a sketch of each of the seven special quadrilaterals: square, rectangle, parallelogram, trapezium, isosceles trapezium, rhombus and kite. If the shape has any lines of symmetry, draw them onto your sketch.

> **Tip**
>
> There are seven quadrilaterals that you use a lot. These are called the special quadrilaterals.

   b Copy and complete this tick box table showing some of the characteristics of the seven special quadrilaterals. The parallelogram has been done for you.

	Quadrilateral						
	Square	Rectangle	Parallelogram	Trapezium	Isosceles trapezium	Rhombus	Kite
Four equal sides							
Two pairs of equal sides			✓				
One pair of equal sides							
One pair of parallel sides							
Two pairs of parallel sides			✓				
All angles 90°							
One pair of equal angles							
Two pairs of equal angles			✓				
Diagonals bisect each other			✓				
Diagonals meet at 90°							

4 Zara and Sofia are looking at this question.

What shape am I?

I am one of the seven special quadrilaterals. I have one pair of equal sides.

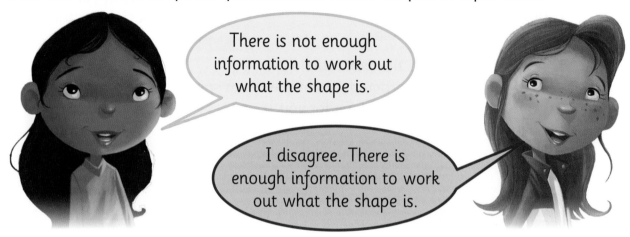

There is not enough information to work out what the shape is.

I disagree. There is enough information to work out what the shape is.

Who is correct, Zara or Sofia? Give a convincing reason to justify your answer.

 5 Keon draws this parallelogram and isosceles trapezium.
He labels the lines that make the shapes a, b, c, d, e, f, g and h.
He draws the shapes so that line a is parallel to line e.

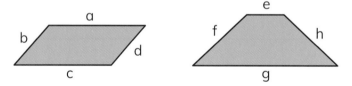

Write true or false for each of these statements. Give a convincing reason to justify your answer. The first one is done for you.

i Line a is parallel to line g

True because we are told line *a* is parallel to line *e* and in the trapezium we know that line *g* is parallel to line *e*, so line *g* must also be parallel to line *a*.

ii Line b is parallel to line d

iii Line c is parallel to line e

iv Line f is parallel to line g

6 This is part of Shen's homework.

Question: Draw a diagram to show if parallelograms tessellate.

Solution: Yes they do. They fit together leaving no spaces.

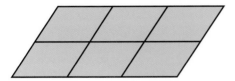 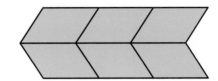

Draw diagrams like Shen's to show, by specialising, if these shapes tessellate.

a rectangle	b rhombus	
c trapezium	d kite	

Tip

Use squared paper to help you.

Think like a mathematician 2

Work with a partner on this activity.

You are going to make a poster showing how you can decompose the special quadrilaterals into other shapes.

For example, three ways that you can decompose a square, are like this:

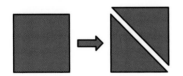 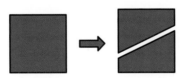 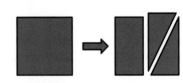

two triangles   two trapezia   a rectangle and two triangles

There are lots of ways to decompose the special quadrilaterals, try to think of at least three for each one.

It is up to you how you present your poster showing the information.

When you have finished, compare your poster with others in your class. Now that you have seen other posters, what do you think of your poster? Could you make it better or easier to understand? Who do you think made the best poster and why?

Look what I can do!

☐ I can identify quadrilaterals.

☐ I can describe quadrilaterals.

☐ I can classify quadrilaterals.

☐ I can sketch quadrilaterals.

❯ 5.2 Circles

We are going to ...

- learn the names of the parts of a circle
- draw circles accurately.

The diagram shows a circle.

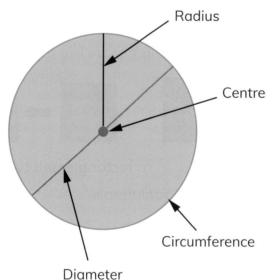

Radius

Centre

Circumference

Diameter

centre	circumference
compasses	diameter
radii	radius

The red dot shows the centre of the circle.

When you draw a circle, you draw a set of points that are the same distance from the centre. This distance is called the radius of the circle.

The perimeter of the circle is called the circumference.

The diameter of the circle is a line joining two points on the circumference that goes through the centre of the circle.

Worked example 2

Draw a circle of radius 4 cm. Label the centre, radius, diameter and circumference of the circle.

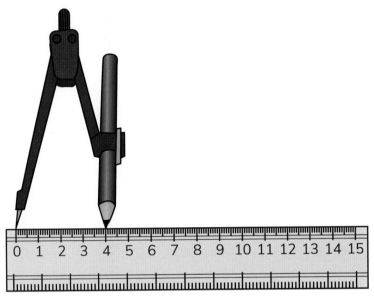

Open your compasses to 4 cm.

Draw a dot to show the centre of the circle, then place the point of your compasses on the dot.

Continued

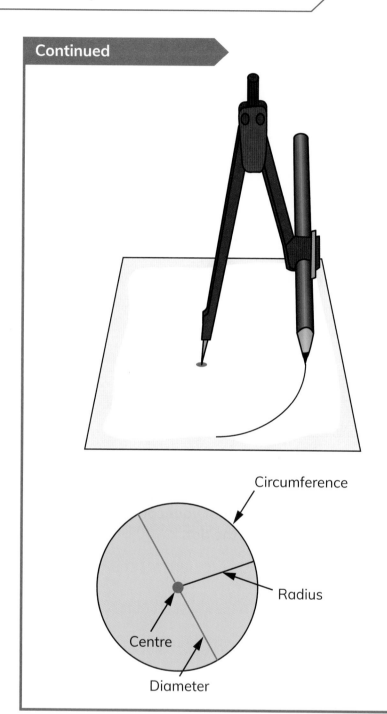

Very carefully turn the compasses to draw the circle.

Circumference

Radius

Centre

Diameter

Draw lines to show the radius and diameter and label the parts of the circle.

Exercise 5.2

1   Copy the diagram. Label the parts of the circle shown using the
    following words: centre, diameter, radius, circumference.

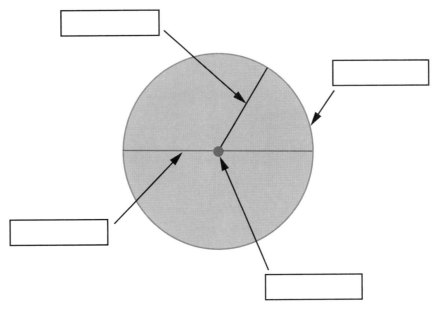

2   Draw a circle with a radius of

    a   5 cm   b   60 mm

Think like a mathematician 1

Arun draws a circle with radius 3 cm.
Sofia draws a circle with diameter 60 mm.
Read what Arun says.

> Our circles
> are exactly the
> same size!

Tip

Remember that
1 cm = 10 mm.

a   Use specialising to decide if Arun is correct. Explain your answer.

b   Write down a general rule that connects the radius
    with the diameter of a circle.

c   Discuss your answers to parts **a** and **b** with
    other learners in your class.

3   These cards show different measurements.

A Radius = 2 cm   B Radius = 10 cm   C Diameter = 8 cm

D Diameter = 20 cm   E Radius = 4 cm   F Radius = 20 mm

G Radius = 40 mm   H Diameter = 4 cm   I Diameter = 200 mm

Classify the cards by organising them into groups of measurements that will give the same size circles.

4   This is part of Gethin's homework.

Task: draw and label a diameter on this circle.

Solution:

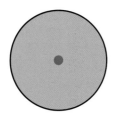

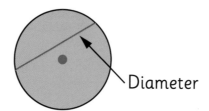

Diameter

a   Explain the mistake that Gethin has made.

b   Draw a correct solution for him.

5   a   Draw a dot and label the point A. Make sure there is about 4 cm of space above, below, to the left and to the right of your point.

b   Draw the set of points that are exactly 3.5 cm from the point A.

Tip

Question 5b means draw a circle of radius 3.5 cm.

6   Ajay, Bryn and Chris are playing on a circular lawn. Name the parts of the circle where they ran.

a   Ajay says 'I ran in a straight line from the edge of the lawn to the centre.'

b   Bryn says 'I ran all the way around the perimeter of the lawn.'

c   Chris says 'I ran in a straight line from one side of the circle, through the centre, to the other side.'

Think like a mathematician 2

a   On a piece of paper, write down

   i   a radius length between 30 mm and 80 mm

   ii   a diameter length between 7 cm and 15 cm.

b   Swap your piece of paper with a partner and ask them to draw
   the two circles with the radius and diameter that you have given.

c   Swap back pieces of paper and mark each other's work.
   How accurate were you and how accurate was your partner?
   If you were not very accurate, discuss ways that you can improve
   the accuracy of your drawings.

Think like a mathematician 3

a   Draw a circle with radius 6 cm. Label the circle A.

b   Draw a circle with radius 2.5 cm, so that it touches circle A. Label the circle B.

   Your diagram should look something like this.

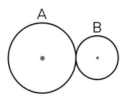

c   With a ruler, accurately measure the
   distance between the centre of circle A and
   the centre of circle B.

> **Tip**
>
> Radii is the plural
> of radius. One
> radius, two radii.

d   What do you notice about your answer to
   part **c** and the radii measurements of
   circles A and B?

e   Draw two more circles that touch. Choose your own radii
   measurements. Measure the distance between the centres of
   your two circles. What do you notice?

f   Copy and complete this general rule:

   The distance between the centres of two touching circles is the

   same as the _____.

Look what I can do!

☐   I can name parts of a circle.

☐   I can draw circles accurately.

> 5.3 Rotational symmetry

We are going to ...

- identify shapes and patterns with rotational symmetry

- describe rotational symmetry.

When you go to a park, you can often play on a swing, a see-saw or a roundabout. Some of the shapes you see will have line symmetry, but have you ever looked at the shapes to see which ones look the same as you turn them?

order

rotational symmetry

A shape has **rotational symmetry** if it can be rotated about a point to another position and still look the same.

The **order** of rotational symmetry is the number of times the shape looks the same in one full turn. A rectangle has rotational symmetry of order 2. This button has rotational symmetry of order 4.

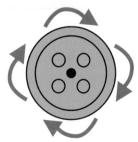

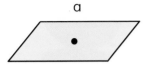

Worked example 3

Fully describe the rotational symmetry of each of these shapes.

a 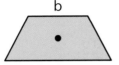   b

a Rotational symmetry order 2	When you rotate the parallelogram about its centre point it looks the same after a half-turn and a full turn, so has order 2.
b Rotational symmetry order 1	When you rotate the isosceles trapezium about its centre point it only looks the same after a full turn so has order 1.

Exercise 5.3

1 Fully describe the rotational symmetry of these shapes.

a   b    c

Tip

You can use tracing paper to help you.

d    e   f

 2 Classify these cards into their correct groups.

Each group must have one rectangle, one circle and one triangle card.

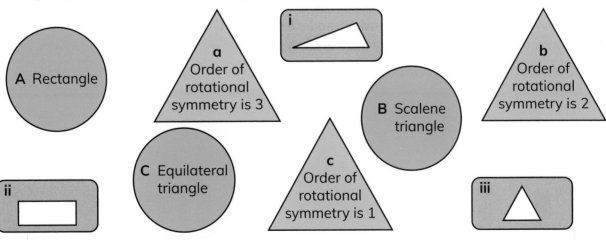

A Rectangle

a Order of rotational symmetry is 3

b Order of rotational symmetry is 2

B Scalene triangle

c Order of rotational symmetry is 1

C Equilateral triangle

i

ii

iii

Think like a mathematician 1

Read what Marcus says.

> A square has 4 lines of symmetry and rotational symmetry order 4. I think that all the special quadrilaterals have the same number of lines of symmetry as order of rotational symmetry.

a   Is Marcus correct? Explain your answer.

b   Is it true to say that a shape with no lines of symmetry will always have rotational symmetry order 1? Explain your answer.

c   Discuss your answer to parts **a** and **b** with other learners in your class.

Think like a mathematician 2

Work with a partner for this activity.

Choose ten capital letters from the alphabet.
For example, you could choose A, E, F, H, K, L, M, N, T and Z.

Work out the number of lines of symmetry and the order of rotational symmetry of your letters.

Make a poster showing your letters; draw on any lines of symmetry and write down the order of rotational symmetry of each letter. Try and choose some letters which have the same, and some letters which have different, numbers of line symmetry and rotational symmetry.

Discuss and compare your posters with other learners in your class.

3   Fully describe the rotational symmetry of these patterns.

a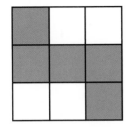

b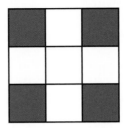

c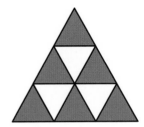

4   Here are four different tiles.

A      B      C      D

a   Write down the order of rotational symmetry of each of the tiles.

b   Juan joins two A tiles together to make this pattern.

What is the order of rotational symmetry of the pattern?

c   Karin joins four B tiles together to make this pattern.

What is the order of rotational symmetry of the pattern?

d   Li joins two C tiles together to make this pattern.

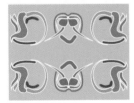

What is the order of rotational symmetry of the pattern?

Work with a partner for this question.

In this section you have found the order of rotational symmetry of shapes and patterns.

a   Explain to your partner the method you find easiest to use to find the order of rotational symmetry of shapes and patterns.

b   Compare your methods. Do you both have the same method? Do you have different methods? Do you think that your method is still the easiest method?

Look what I can do!

☐   I can identify shapes and patterns with rotational symmetry.

☐   I can describe rotational symmetry.

Check your progress

1   Write down the missing numbers from each of these statements.

a   A square has _____ equal sides.

b   A parallelogram has _____ pairs of parallel sides.

c   The diagonals of a kite meet at _____°.

d   An isosceles trapezium has _____ pair of equal sides.

e   A rectangle has _____ lines of symmetry.

f   A rhombus has _____ pairs of equal angles.

2   a   Draw a circle of radius 2.5 cm.

b   Label the centre, circumference, a radius and a diameter on the circle.

3   Write down the order of rotational symmetry of each of these road signs.

a   b   c   d

❀ ⟩ Project 3

Petal problems

In this picture, a ladybird is sitting on a petal of a flower. This picture only has rotational symmetry of order 1, because when we rotate it about the centre it only looks the same as this after a full turn.

> Copy the picture. Can you draw another ladybird on this flower so that it has rotational symmetry of order 2?
>
> What other orders of rotational symmetry could this flower have? Can you draw more ladybirds on the flower to show the different possibilities?

There is a ladybird sitting on one petal of each of these flowers.

> For each flower, copy the picture then draw some more ladybirds to change the order of rotational symmetry.
>
> Can you add ladybirds to one of these flowers so that it has rotational symmetry of order 3?
>
> What about rotational symmetry of order 4? Order 6?
>
> How would you convince someone else that the flower has that particular order of rotational symmetry?

Getting started

1   Maria eats $\frac{5}{8}$ of a chocolate bar with mass 240 g.

How many grams of chocolate does Maria eat?

2   What part of each diagram is shaded?

Write each answer as a percentage and as a fraction with a denominator of 100.

a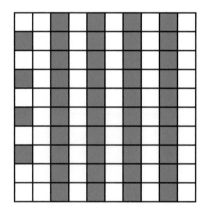

b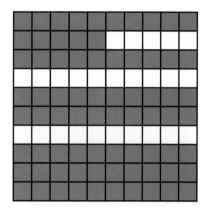

c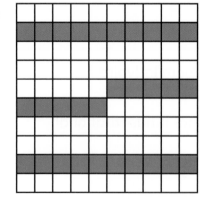

3   Use each of the digits 4 and 5 once to complete these number sentences.

4.8 > ☐ .5   4.8 < ☐ .5

Continued

4 Write these fractions, decimals and percentages in order starting with the smallest.

$\frac{3}{4}$ 0.2 $\frac{1}{4}$ 70%   0.3

5 Use each of the digits 1, 5, 0 and 2 once to complete this statement.

$\frac{2}{10}$ = $\frac{\boxed{}}{\boxed{}}$ = $\boxed{}$ • $\boxed{}$

When do we use percentages?

Here are some examples.

What is your favourite sport?

Swimming 10%
Basketball 40%
Hockey 20%
Football 30%

I scored 70% in the maths test!

There is a 30% chance of rain today.

SUMMER SALE 10-50% OFF EVERYTHING!

Can you think of other times we use percentages?

This unit is all about fractions, decimals and percentages.

> 6.1 Understanding fractions

We are going to ...

- represent a proper or improper fraction as a division

- use proper and improper fractions as operators.

An improper fraction represents a number greater than or equal to 1 whole.

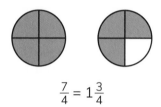

$$\frac{7}{4} = 1\frac{3}{4}$$

denominator

improper fraction

mixed number

numerator

operator

proper fraction

For example, this diagram shows the improper fraction $\frac{7}{4}$.

This is equal to $1\frac{3}{4}$ which is a mixed number.

In this unit we will work with proper fractions, improper fractions and mixed numbers.

Tip

Remember, that > means 'greater than' and < means 'less than'.

Worked example 1

Which is bigger $\frac{3}{4}$ of 20 or $\frac{4}{3}$ of 12?

Explain how you know.

$\frac{3}{4}$ of 20 = $3 \times \frac{1}{4}$ of 20

$= 3 \times 5 = 15$

$\frac{4}{3}$ of 12 = $4 \times \frac{1}{3}$ of 12

$= 4 \times 4 = 16$

So $\frac{4}{3}$ of 12 $> \frac{3}{4}$ of 20

You can also work out $\frac{3}{4}$ of 20

by calculating $20 \div 4 \times 3 = 15$.

$\frac{4}{3}$ of 12 is equivalent to $12 \div 3 \times 4$.

Exercise 6.1

1   Represent these divisions as fractions.

    a   5 divided by 6   b   6 divided by 5

    c   10 divided by 4   d   4 divided by 10

2   Ahmed, Carlos, Ludvik, Oliver and Rajiv share 3 cakes equally between them.

    What fraction of a cake does each person get?

3   Which word can you use to complete this sentence?

    When you find $\frac{6}{5}$ of a number you are using a fraction as an _____ .

4   Calculate.

    a $\frac{3}{4}$ of \$16   b $\frac{5}{4}$ of \$12   c $\frac{5}{2}$ of 4 metres

5   Halima swims $\frac{1}{2}$ of 500 metres and Bella swims $\frac{3}{10}$ of 800 metres.

    Who swims further? Explain how you know.

6   Leroy and Wayne each have 90 bricks.

    Leroy uses $\frac{3}{5}$ of his bricks to build a wall.

    Wayne uses $\frac{5}{6}$ of his bricks to build a wall.

    How many bricks do they have left altogether? Show your working.

    Discuss your answer with your partner. Do you agree?

Look back at your answers to questions **5** and **6** where you had to explain and show your working.
What improvements can you make? Discuss your ideas with your partner.

7   Copy and complete this table to show fractions of 24.

Fraction	$\frac{1}{4}$	$\frac{3}{4}$	$\frac{5}{4}$	$\frac{7}{4}$	$\frac{9}{4}$	$\frac{11}{4}$
Amount	6					

8   Calculate.

a $\frac{9}{4}$ of 16   b $\frac{7}{5}$ of 35   c $\frac{8}{7}$ of 14   d $\frac{4}{3}$ of 15

Think like a mathematician

Imagine that you roll two 1–6 dice and use them to make an improper fraction.

$\frac{5}{3}$ is an improper fraction

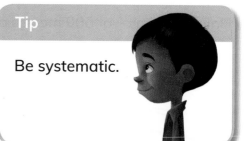

Tip

Be systematic.

Write all the different improper fractions you could make.

You will show you are **specialising** when you find different improper fractions.

9   Write all the numbers from this list that give the result of dividing 23 by 5.

$4\frac{6}{10}$ 4.6 $4\frac{3}{10}$ $4\frac{3}{5}$ $\frac{23}{5}$ 4.3

10 Which of these representations are equivalent to $\frac{48}{5}$?

5 ÷ 48   9.3 $9\frac{3}{5}$ 48 ÷ 5   9.6

Look what I can do!

☐   I can represent a proper or improper fraction as a division.

☐   I can use proper and improper fractions as operators.

› 6.2 Percentages

We are going to ...

- find percentages of whole numbers and shapes.

Have you ever seen a shop that is having a sale?

Sometimes shops will offer an amount off the price, for example, $5 off.

More often though they offer a percentage off, for example, 10% off or 25% off.

operator

per cent

percentage

If a jumper originally costs $20, but a 10% reduction is offered, how much money is taken off in the sale?

Worked example 2

Find 20% of these quantities.

a   50   b   20 cm   c $30   d   110 kg

a   10% is 5 so 20% is 10

b   10% is 2 cm so 20% is 4 cm

c   10% is $3 so 20% is $6

d   10% is 11 kg so 20% is 22 kg

$10\% = \frac{1}{10}$ so to find 10% divide by 10.

Multiply the result by 2 to find 20%.

Remember to write the units in the answer.

Exercise 6.2

1 Find 10% of these quantities.

   a   40   b   70 cm   c $20   d   120 kg

2 A man has a mass of 80 kg. 60% of his total mass is water.
   What is the mass of this water?

 3 Helga says, 'To calculate 10% of a quantity, you divide it by 10,
   so to find 50%, you divide by 5.'

   Helga is not correct. Explain what is wrong with her statement.

4 What percentage of the diagram is shaded?

5 What percentage of each diagram is shaded?

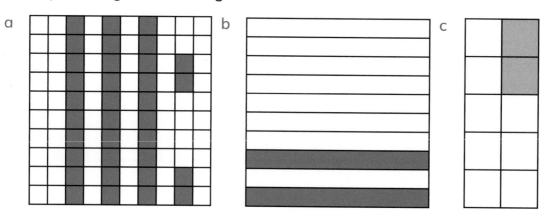

6 Calculate.

   a   15% of 120   b   45% of 240   c   65% of 180

Check your answers to questions **5** and **6** with your partner.

7 Amy has $400. She spends 40% of her money on a new bike.

   How much does she spend on the bike?

8 Song has a strip of paper 20 cm long.

   He cuts a 5 cm piece off the strip.

   What percentage of the strip does he cut off?

9 a A coat originally cost $40. The price goes up by 10%.
What is the new price?

b A garden centre sells plants at 25% off at the end of the month.
The price of a plant was originally $8. What is its price at the
end of the month?

10 The pie chart shows the favourite animals of a group of Stage 6 children.

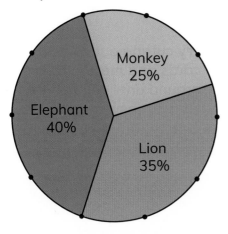

Tip

A pie chart shows a
divided circle where each
section represents a
percentage of the total.
In this diagram 40% of the
children chose elephants.

32 children chose elephants.

How many children are in the Stage 6 group? Explain your answer.

In questions **3** and **10** you had to write an explanation.
Did you find that easy or hard? If you found it hard,
try explaining answers to your partner first and then
work together to write down your thoughts.

Think like a mathematician

Here are twelve numbers.

10　20　25　40　50　60

75　100　150　160　500　600

Can you write four number sentences using each of the twelve numbers once?

▢ % of ▢ is ▢　　▢ % of ▢ is ▢

▢ % of ▢ is ▢　　▢ % of ▢ is ▢

You will show you are **specialising** when you find solutions to the problem.

Tip

Try cutting out number cards and moving them around until you find the correct answer.

Look what I can do!

☐　I can find percentages of whole numbers and shapes.

> 6.3 Equivalence and comparison

We are going to ...

- reduce fractions to their simplest form

- recognise that fractions, decimals and percentages can have equivalent values

- compare fractions, decimals and percentages using the symbols =, > and <

- order fractions, decimals and percentages.

You can simplify a fraction if you can divide both the numerator and denominator by the same number.

$$\underset{\div 2}{\overset{\div 2}{\frac{4}{20}}} = \underset{\div 2}{\overset{\div 2}{\frac{2}{10}}} = \frac{1}{5} \qquad \underset{\div 5}{\overset{\div 5}{\frac{5}{25}}} = \frac{1}{5}$$

> equivalent fractions
> simplest form   simplify a fraction

$\frac{1}{5}$ is the simplest form of the fraction.

You will learn how to simplify fractions in this section.

Worked example 3

Kiki says $\frac{7}{10}$ is equivalent to 10.7

Davy says $\frac{7}{10}$ is equivalent to 0.7

Mohammed says $\frac{7}{10}$ is equivalent to 1.07

Do you agree with any of these students?

Explain your answer.

Davy gave the correct answer.

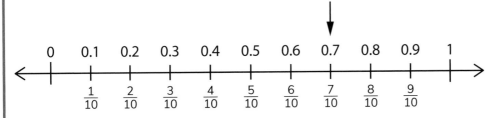

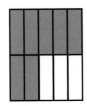 $\frac{7}{10}$ $\frac{7}{10} = 0.7$

The digit 7 in 0.7 represents 7 tenths.

$\frac{7}{10}$ is less than one whole.

Mohammed and Kiki have included a whole number which is incorrect.

Exercise 6.3

1   What fraction of the shape is shaded?

Write your answer in its simplest form.

2   Write these fractions in their simplest form.

a $\dfrac{4}{16}$ b $\dfrac{12}{20}$ c $\dfrac{18}{24}$

3   Here are six number cards.

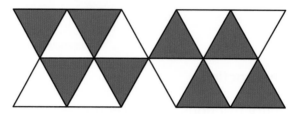

Use four of these cards to complete the number sentence.

$\dfrac{1}{4} = \dfrac{\Box}{\Box} = \dfrac{\Box}{\Box}$

Which of the three fractions is in the simplest form?

4   Write these numbers in their simplest form.

a $\dfrac{12}{8}$ b $\dfrac{20}{16}$ c $1\dfrac{4}{10}$

Check your answers with your partner.

5   Here are three statements about fractions and percentages.

Which statements are true?

Which statements are not true? Correct these statements.

A $\dfrac{3}{100}$ is equal to 3%   B $\dfrac{4}{5}$ is equal to 45%   C $\dfrac{7}{10}$ is equal to 7%

6   Which two fractions are equal to 0.6?

$\dfrac{1}{6}$ $\dfrac{60}{100}$ $\dfrac{1}{60}$ $\dfrac{6}{10}$

7   Copy and complete this table to show equivalent values.

Fraction	Decimal	Percentage
$\dfrac{57}{100}$		
		8%
	1.25	

8   Write these fractions in order starting with the smallest fraction.

a $\dfrac{1}{4}$ $\dfrac{5}{8}$ $\dfrac{1}{8}$ $\dfrac{3}{4}$ $\dfrac{3}{8}$

b $\dfrac{7}{12}$ $\dfrac{3}{4}$ $\dfrac{1}{2}$ $\dfrac{5}{6}$ $\dfrac{2}{3}$

9   Write these numbers in order starting with the largest.

7.7   7.07   7.77   7.17   7.71

10 Use one of the symbols <, > or = to make each statement correct.

$\dfrac{7}{10}$ ☐ 0.07

23% ☐ 0.23

75% ☐ $\dfrac{4}{5}$

11 Anil says, '0.25 is smaller than $\dfrac{2}{5}$.' Is Anil correct? Explain your answer.

12 Write these numbers in order, starting with the smallest.

$\dfrac{7}{10}$ 50%   0.65 $\dfrac{3}{5}$

Think about the work you have covered in this unit.
You have learned about fractions, decimals and percentages.
Do you find it easier to work with fractions or decimals or
percentages? What do you need to get better at?

Think like a mathematician

Imagine you spin both these spinners to make a fraction.

Investigate how many different fractions you can make.

Write all the proper fractions as percentages.

Write all the improper fractions as decimal numbers.

Order the decimals and percentages starting with the largest number.

You will show you can **classify** when you sort the fractions into proper and improper fractions.

numerator   denominator

Example: 5 and 4 gives $\frac{5}{4}$

Look what I can do!

- ☐ I can reduce fractions to their simplest form.
- ☐ I can recognise fractions, decimals and percentages that have equivalent values.
- ☐ I can compare fractions, decimals and percentages using the symbols =, > and <.
- ☐ I can order fractions, decimals and percentages.

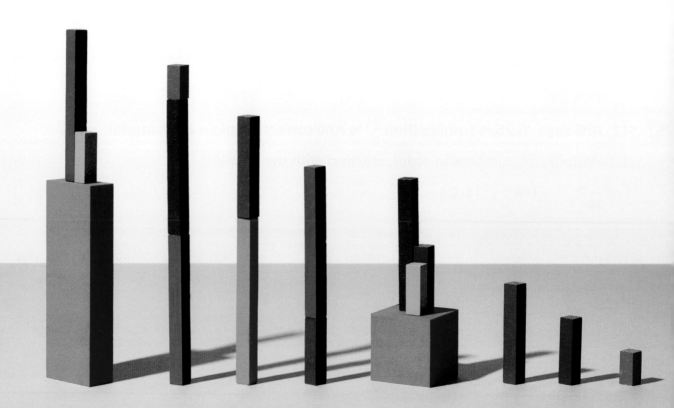

6.3 Equivalence and comparison

Check your progress

1 Which is bigger $\frac{3}{4}$ of 40 or $\frac{4}{3}$ of 24?

   Explain how you know.

2 Write $\frac{24}{32}$ in its simplest form.

3 Write these numbers in order of size, starting with the smallest.

   66% $\frac{3}{5}$ 0.42   55% $\frac{9}{20}$

4 There are 20 big cats in a safari park.

A pie chart showing the percentage of big cats in the park

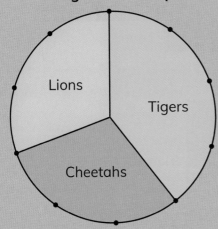

> **Tip**
>
> You can use the dots on the circumference of the circle to help you divide the circle into 10 equal parts.

   a Which statements are true?

      A   40% of the big cats are tigers.

      B   There are more lions than cheetahs.

      C $\frac{3}{10}$ of the big cats are lions

   b What percentage of the big cats are cheetahs?

   c How many tigers are at the zoo?

7 Exploring measures

1 Work out the area and the perimeter of each shape.

a

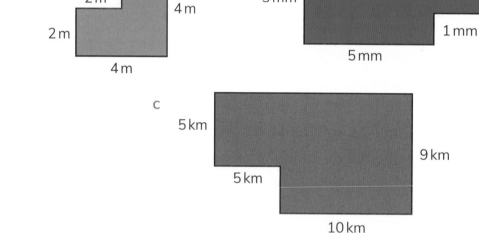

2 m
2 m
2 m
2 m
2 m
4 m
4 m

b

10 mm
3 mm
2 mm
1 mm
5 mm

c

5 km
5 km
9 km
10 km

2 These clocks show the wrong time. What time should each clock show?
Answer using digital clock notation.

a It is the evening and this clock is
1 hour and 10 minutes slow.

b It is the morning and this clock
is 3 and a half hours fast.

Measures are ways that we practically apply mathematics in solving problems, investigating and in everyday life.

What could you measure and what problems could you solve with each of these objects?

> 7.1 Rectangles and triangles

We are going to ...

- estimate the area of a triangle

- work out the area of triangles using rectangles.

A 1 kg bag of grass seed covers 20 m² of ground.

How would you measure or calculate how many bags you would buy to cover a large field?

Explain to a partner how you would decide on the number of bags.

area

Tip

Remember that a square is a type of rectangle.

Exercise 7.1

1   This rectangle was made by putting two squares together.

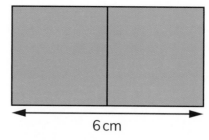

6 cm

   a   What is the area of the rectangle?

   b   What is the area of one of the squares?

2   This square was made by putting two identical rectangles together.

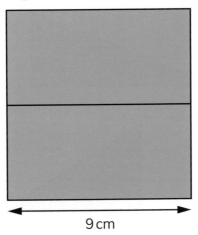

9 cm

a   What is the area of the square?

b   What is the area of one of the rectangles?

3   Asok took two pieces of paper.

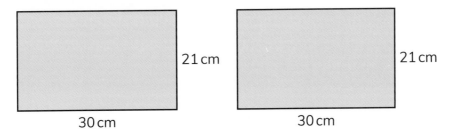

21 cm   21 cm

30 cm   30 cm

He cut one piece of paper in half, like picture A.   A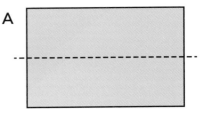

a   What was the area of the piece of paper before it
was cut?

b   What is the area of one of the smaller pieces of paper
Asok made?

He cut the other piece of paper in half, like picture B.   B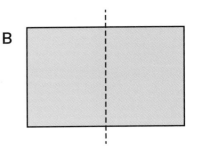

c   What is the area of one of the smaller pieces of paper
Asok made?

4 Estimate the area of these triangles by counting the squares.

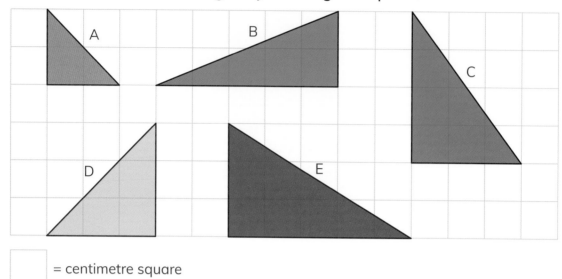

☐ = centimetre square

What knowledge are you using about squares to help you decide if a square is half covered by a shape? What different ways do you think a square can be cut into two equal pieces with a straight line? Talk to a partner about your ideas.

5 Selena made this pattern by overlapping tissue paper triangles.

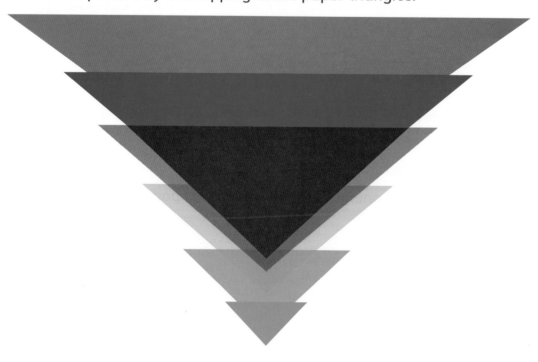

Here are the bottom three triangles, as they look on a centimetre square grid.

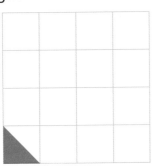 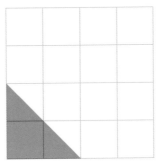 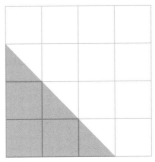

= centimetre square

a   Draw and complete a table to show the area of each triangle in the pattern.

b   What would be the area of the 7th triangle?

c   What would be the area of the 10th triangle?

d   Look at the pattern of numbers in your table.
    Try to describe the pattern of the areas of the triangles.

    Can you think of a way to always predict what the area of the next triangle will be?

    Generalise by describing the link between the number of each triangle and its area.

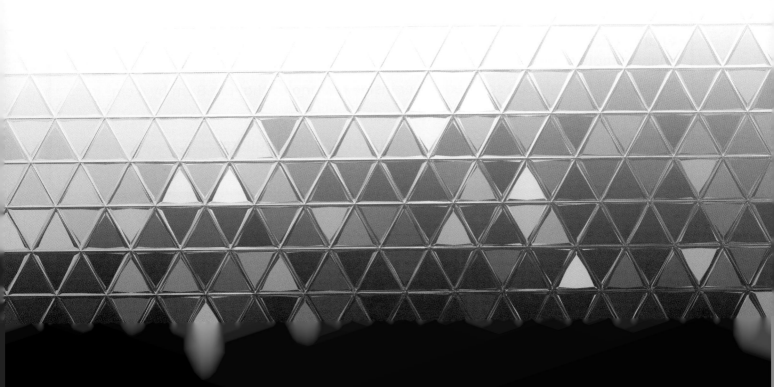

Think like a mathematician

What is the area of each of these rectangles?

Each triangle is drawn on centimetre squared paper.
Count squares to estimate the area of each triangle.

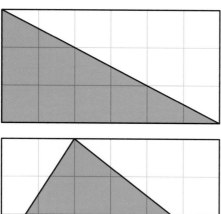
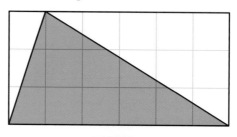

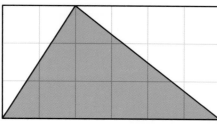
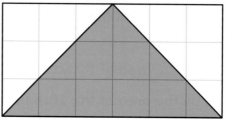

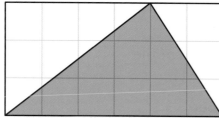
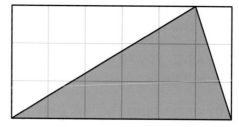

 = centimetre square

Characterise by describing what you notice about the area of the triangles from your estimates.

Draw more triangles on squared paper inside rectangles that are 8 cm by 4 cm.

Each triangle should be as wide and as tall as the rectangle.

Estimate the area of the triangles you draw by counting squares.

Generalise by describing what you find out.

Worked example 1

This rectangle has been cut in half to make two triangles.

What is the area of each blue triangle in this rectangle?

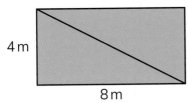

Work out the area of the whole rectangle.

The area of the rectangle is 32 m².

Divide the area in half.

32 ÷ 2 = 16.

Don't forget to use units of area. The lengths are in metres so the area will be m².

Each triangle has an area of 16 m².

Multiply the width by the length to find the area of a rectangle.

Each of the triangles is half of the rectangle.

Units of area include mm², cm², m² and km².

6 These rectangles are cut in half diagonally to make two triangles.

For each diagram work out the area of the rectangle and the area of one of the triangles.

a

b

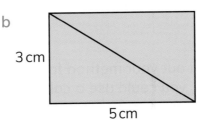

c

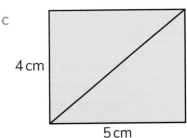

d

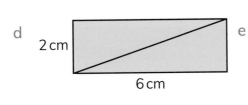

e

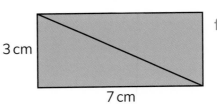

f

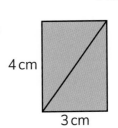

7   Work out the area of the rectangle.

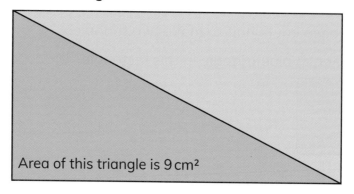

Area of this triangle is 9 cm²

8   Jo makes triangular biscuits by cutting out 5 cm squares of dough, then cutting them in half.

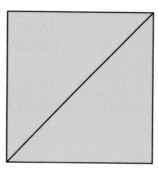

Jo wants to cover each biscuit in icing.

This tub of icing covers 340 cm² of biscuit.

How many triangular biscuits will Jo be able to cover?

Biscuit icing

Tip

Once you have worked out your method for finding the number of biscuits, you could use a calculator for the calculations. Don't forget to interpret the answer on the calculator in the context of the question.

Look what I can do!

☐   I can estimate the area of a triangle.

☐   I can work out the area of triangles using rectangles.

› 7.2 Time

We are going to ...

- convert between time intervals expressed as a decimal and in mixed units.

Calculating times can be tricky because units of time do not usually come in 10s and 100s.

Look at each of these numbers.
What does each number have to do with time?

60   12

365   30

100   7   366

24

Why do the different units in time make it more tricky to calculate with time?

Worked example 2

Convert 3.7 hours into hours and minutes.

3.7 hours =

3 whole hours + 0.7 of an hour

Either	There are 60 minutes in 1 hour so there are 0.7 × 60 minutes in 0.7 of an hour.
0.7 × 60 = 42	
Or	0.1 (one tenth) of an hour equals 6 minutes, so 0.7 (seven tenths) of an hour equals 7 × 6 minutes.
7 × 6 = 42	

3.7 hours = 3 hours and 42 minutes

Exercise 7.2

1   Copy and complete the table to show times in hours and in hours and minutes.

Hours	Hours and minutes	Hours	Hours and minutes
0.1 hours	0 hours and 6 minutes	0.8 hours	
0.2 hours	0 hours and __ minutes	0.9 hours	
0.3 hours		1 hour	
0.4 hours		1.1 hours	
0.5 hours		2.2 hours	
0.6 hours		3.8 hours	
0.7 hours		4.9 hours	

2   4 children are allowed to share a games console for 5 hours. They decide to divide the 5 hours equally between them.

> **Tip**
>
> You could use a calculator to divide the number of hours by the number of children.

a   How much time does each child get on the games console in hours?

b   Tom says that each child can have 1 hour and 25 minutes on the console. Tom is wrong. Explain why Tom is wrong and work out how many hours and minutes each child can have on the console.

Reflect on why you think Tom made this mistake. What will you do to make sure that you do not make the same mistake when interpreting and converting times?

3 Ten athletes competed in a marathon run.

These are their times:

Gianmarco	159.1 minutes
Yared	141.7 minutes
Emily	182.8 minutes
Emmanuel	128.65 minutes
Maria	183.05 minutes

Mai	174.3 minutes
Susan	158.9 minutes
Florence	141.55 minutes
Paul	129.25 minutes
Kazuyoshi	135.45 minutes

Copy the table below.

List the runners in the table from fastest to slowest.

Convert each of their times into hours, minutes and seconds and complete the table with the converted times.

Runner	Hours	Minutes	Seconds

Think like a mathematician

You know that 12.5 hours is not equal to 12 hours and 5 minutes.

Are there any times in hours that use the same digits as the same amount of time in hours and minutes?

Specialise by choosing particular times to check.

Generalise by writing a statement explaining what you have found out.

Look what I can do!

☐ I can convert between time intervals expressed as a decimal and in mixed units.

Check your progress

1   Count the squares to estimate the area of these triangles.

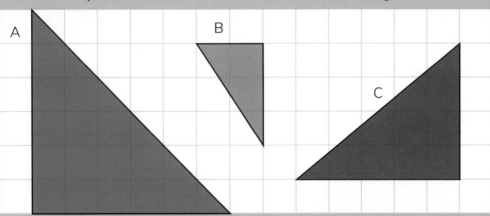

 = centimetre square

2   Measure the lengths of the sides of these rectangles to work out the area of these triangles.

a 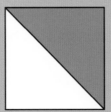   b 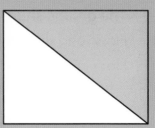   c

Continued

3   Harry is covering one of the triangular areas of his garden with grass seed.
    Which is the smallest bag of seeds he can buy to cover the area?

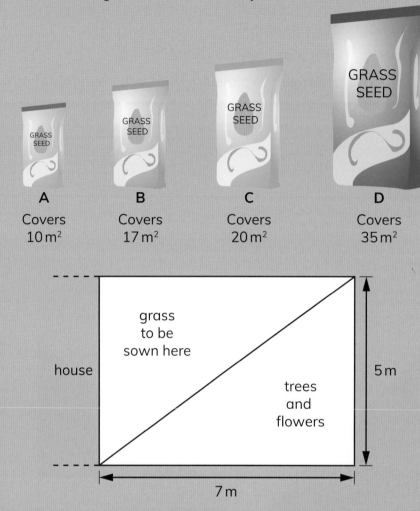

A

Covers
10 m²

B

Covers
17 m²

C

Covers
20 m²

D

Covers
35 m²

4   Write these times as hours and minutes.

   a   3.5 hours   **b**   14.1 hours   **c**   9.25 hours

   d   5.7 hours   **e**   11.4 hours   **f**   1.05 hours

5   5 groups wanted to use a basketball court. The court was open for 12 hours.
    The groups shared the 12 hours between the groups equally.

    How long did each group get on the court in hours?

    How long did each group get on the court in hours and minutes?

🌀 › Project 4

Ordering times

Put these lengths of time in order, from shortest to longest.
You might like to use a calculator to help you.

A second	Time since you were born	A thousand seconds	A decade
Time for light to reach the Earth from the Sun	A minute	Time it takes you to eat a meal	100 000 hours
1000 months	A century	A day	Time it takes you to say the alphabet
A month	1000 days	Time since the last Olympic Games	A fortnight
Time it takes the Moon to go once around the Earth	A year	5 000 000 minutes	Time since the invention of the telephone

How did you choose what order to put them in?

Did you have to estimate any that you weren't sure about?
How could you work out exactly how long each of these takes?

Did your partner put them in the same order as you, or did they choose a different order? Why?

8 ▶ Addition and subtraction (2)

Getting started

1 What is the value of the digit 5 in 3.56?

2 Write this as a decimal number:

$$3 + 10 + \frac{3}{100} + \frac{1}{10}$$

3 Stefan is 1.4 metres tall. Yuri is 1.2 metres tall.
   How much taller is Stefan than Yuri?

4 a What is the sum of 65.98 and 32.75?

   b What is the difference between 54.31 and 46.76?

5 Calculate.

   a $\frac{3}{5} + \frac{4}{5}$

   b $\frac{9}{8} - \frac{5}{8}$

   c $\frac{4}{5} - \frac{3}{10}$

6 Anita spent $\frac{1}{6}$ of her money on a dress and $\frac{2}{3}$ of her money on a coat.
   What fraction of her money did she spend altogether?

We use addition and subtraction in many different situations, such as when shopping.

Can you think of other situations where we use addition and subtraction?

In this unit, you will learn more about addition and subtraction, including using fractions and decimals.

› 8.1 Adding and subtracting decimal numbers

We are going to ...

- compose, decompose and regroup decimals with up to 3 decimal places
- estimate, add and subtract numbers with the same or different numbers of decimal places.

Usain Bolt broke the world record for the 100 metres in 2009 by running it in 9.58 seconds.

The qualifying time for the 2020 Olympics was 10.05 seconds.

What is the difference in these two times?

To work out this answer, you need to subtract. In this section, you will learn more about adding and subtracting decimals.

decimal place

Worked example 1

Jyoti buys two toy cars.

$4.49

$3.09

She pays with a $10 note.

How much change does she get?

Estimate:

Estimate the answer.

4 + 3 = 7 and 10 − 7 = 3 so the answer will be close to $3.

Continued

Add 4.49 and 3.09 to get 7.58 then subtract 7.58 from 10.

Method 1 uses regrouping.

Method 1:

4.49 ➤ 4 + 0.4 + 0.09

+ 3.09 ➤ 3   + 0.09

7 + 0.4 + 0.18 = 7.58

Write 10 as 9 + 0.9 + 0.10

10.00 ➤ 9 + 0.9 + 0.10

– 7.58 ➤ 7 + 0.5 + 0.08

2 + 0.4 + 0.02 = 2.42

Method 2:

$$
\begin{array}{r}
4\,.\,49 \\
+\,3\,.\,09 \\
\hline
7\,.\,58 \\
\hline
1
\end{array}
\qquad
\begin{array}{r}
9\quad9\ 1 \\
\cancel{10}\,.\,\cancel{0}\ 0 \\
-\quad7\,.\,58 \\
\hline
2\,.\,42
\end{array}
$$

Method 2 uses a compact method of recording. Remember to use trailing zeros so all numbers have the same number of decimal places.

Answer: Jyoti gets $2.42 change.

Check your answer against the estimate. Write the answer in dollars.

Exercise 8.1

1 Which of the following is equivalent to 6.075?

A 6 + 0.7 + 0.5   B 6 + 0.7 + 0.05

C 6 + 0.07 + 0.05   D 6 + 0.07 + 0.005

2 Write the missing numbers.

37.844 = 30 + 7 + ☐ + 0.04 + ☐

3 Which two numbers have a total of 1?

0.80   0.08   0.88   0.02   0.12   0.22

4 Find the sum of all the numbers less than 5.5 in this list.

5.05   5.55   5.115   5.5   5.555

5 Calculate:

a 14.8 + 5.678

b 13.26 + 17.604

c 45.83 + 31.104

d 56.1 – 26.64

e 68.603 – 52.75

f 70.394 – 49.78

Did you remember to estimate? Explain to your partner how you estimated and worked out the answers.

6 Ahmed calculates: 0.7 + 0.41 = 0.48.

He has made a mistake. How can you help him avoid making the same mistake again?

7 Calculate 1.4 + 2.56 – 3.789.

8 Mike and Long dig up potatoes.

Mike digs up 8.45 kilograms of potatoes.

Long digs up 10.5 kilograms of potatoes.

How many kilograms of potatoes do they dig up altogether?

> **Tip**
>
> Always remember to estimate before you calculate.

9 Some children are collecting money for a charity.

Their target is $350. They have collected $158.73 so far.

How much more money do they need to reach their target?

10 Darius packs two suitcases to take on a plane.

One suitcase weighs 11.284 kg. The other weighs 8.65 kg.

Darius is allowed to take 20 kg of luggage on the plane. How much are his suitcases under the 20 kg limit?

Look back at your work. Did you use the worked example to help you? Did you find it helpful to discuss your answers with your partner? How can you improve your work?

Think like a mathematician

Arrange the digits 0, 1, 2, 3, 4, 5, 6 and 7 to make two numbers with 3 decimal places. Do not use 0 in the ones or the thousandths place.

 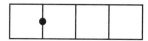

- Find the sum closest to 4.
- Find the difference closest to 1.

You will show you are **specialising** when you find solutions to the problems.

Look what I can do!

☐ I can compose, decompose and regroup decimals with up to 3 decimal places.

☐ I can estimate, add and subtract numbers with the same or different numbers of decimal places.

› 8.2 Adding and subtracting fractions

We are going to …

- add and subtract two fractions with different denominators.

Two pizzas of equal size are delivered to a family.

The cheese and tomato pizza is divided into 8 pieces.

common denominator

denominator

The special pizza is divided into 5 pieces.

Tarik eats 3 pieces of the cheese and tomato pizza and one piece of the special pizza. What fraction of a whole pizza does Tarik eat?

We can use fractions to work this out.

In this unit, you will learn how to add and subtract fractions with different denominators. As with all calculations, it is good practice to estimate your answer before working it out. This will give you a sense of the size of the fraction to expect.

Worked example 2

Calculate $\dfrac{9}{5} + \dfrac{3}{4}$

Estimate: a fraction equal to between 2 and 3

First estimate your answer. $\dfrac{9}{5}$ is nearly 2, and $\dfrac{3}{4}$ is less than 1, so we would expect a fraction that is larger than 2 but less than 3.

Multiples of 5: 5, 10, 15, 20, ...

Multiples of 4: 4, 8, 12, 16, 20, ...

Find a common denominator by looking at multiples of 5 and 4.

$\dfrac{9}{5} = \dfrac{36}{20}$

$\dfrac{3}{4} = \dfrac{15}{20}$

Change $\dfrac{9}{5}$ and $\dfrac{3}{4}$ to equivalent fractions with a denominator of 20.

$\dfrac{9}{5} + \dfrac{3}{4} = \dfrac{36}{20} + \dfrac{15}{20}$

Add the numerators.

$= \dfrac{51}{20}$

Simplify if possible.

Change improper fractions to mixed numbers.

$= 2\dfrac{11}{20}$

Check back against your estimate. $2\dfrac{11}{20}$ is between 2 and 3, so this looks correct.

Think like a mathematician 1

Which is bigger? $\dfrac{3}{7}$ or $\dfrac{4}{9}$.

Explain your answer to a partner.

You will show you are **convincing** when you explain your reasoning to your partner.

Exercise 8.2

1 Copy and complete the table.

Calculation	Common denominator	Equivalent calculation	Answer
$\frac{1}{3}+\frac{1}{6}$			
$\frac{7}{10}-\frac{1}{2}$			
$\frac{6}{5}+\frac{1}{2}$			

2 Calculate.

a $\frac{3}{4}+\frac{2}{5}$

b $\frac{5}{8}-\frac{1}{3}$

c $\frac{7}{8}+\frac{3}{5}$

3 Find the missing fractions.

$\frac{7}{4}-\frac{4}{5}=$ ☐

☐ $+\frac{2}{3}=\frac{13}{4}$

Check your answers to questions **2** and **3** with your partner.

4 Chipo and Leke work out the answer to $\frac{2}{3}+\frac{3}{5}$.

Chipo says the answer is $\frac{19}{15}$.

Leke says the answer is $1\frac{4}{15}$.

Who do you agree with? Explain your answer.

5 Calculate.

a $\frac{3}{2}+\frac{4}{5}$

b $\frac{11}{4}+\frac{5}{3}$

c $\frac{9}{8}+\frac{2}{3}$

6 Calculate.

a $\frac{5}{2}-\frac{3}{5}$

b $\frac{11}{4}-\frac{5}{3}$

c $\frac{8}{3}-\frac{4}{5}$

7 Leroy colours $\frac{1}{4}$ and $\frac{1}{6}$ of a circle.

What fraction of the circle does he leave white?

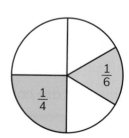

8   Nailah's class voted for where to go on the school outing.

$\frac{3}{4}$ of the class voted for the theme park.

$\frac{2}{9}$ of the class voted for the zoo.

The rest of the class voted for a river trip.
What fraction of the class voted for the river trip?

9   Jo plants potatoes, carrots and onions in her vegetable garden.

She plants potatoes in $\frac{2}{3}$ of her garden.

She plants carrots in $\frac{1}{4}$ of her garden.

What fraction of her garden does
she plant with onions?

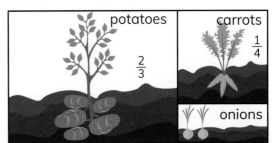

potatoes   carrots

$\frac{1}{4}$

$\frac{2}{3}$

Not to
scale

onions

Look back over the questions in this exercise.
What can you do to improve your work?

Think like a mathematician 2

Copy and complete the table.

$\frac{1}{5} + \frac{1}{2} = \frac{7}{10}$	$\frac{1}{5} + \frac{1}{3} = \frac{8}{15}$	$\frac{1}{5} + \frac{1}{4} = \frac{9}{20}$	$\frac{1}{5} + \frac{1}{5} = \frac{10}{25}$		
$\frac{1}{7} + \frac{1}{2} = \frac{9}{14}$	$\frac{1}{7} + \frac{1}{3} = \frac{10}{21}$	$\frac{1}{7} + \frac{1}{4} = ?$			
$\frac{1}{9} + \frac{1}{2} = \frac{11}{18}$	$\frac{1}{9} + \frac{1}{3} = ?$	$\frac{1}{9} + \frac{1}{4} = ?$			

Can you find a rule for your patterns? You can write your rule in words or in symbols.

You will show you are **generalising** when you find a rule for your patterns.

Look what I can do!

☐ I can add and subtract two fractions with different denominators.

Check your progress

1 Find the value of $\frac{13}{4} + \frac{7}{3}$.

2 a What is the total of 4.79 and 5.306?

   b What is the difference between 4.79 and 7.428?

   c What is the difference between $\frac{5}{3}$ and $\frac{9}{8}$?

3 Parveen creates a spice mixture using ginger, garlic and chilli.

$\frac{2}{5}$ of the mixture is ginger.

$\frac{1}{6}$ of the mixture is garlic.

What fraction of the mixture is chilli?

4 Find the missing digits to make this calculation correct.

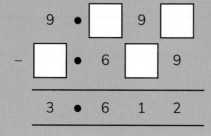

9 ▶ Probability

Getting started

1   Choose the best position for each of these events on the likelihood scale.
    Write the reason for each choice.

    impossible   unlikely   even   likely   certain
                                      chance

    A   You will have a bath this week.

    B   You will be dressed by 8 a.m. tomorrow.

    C   You will live to be 200 years old.

    D   You will go to the Moon next year.

    E   You will listen to the radio today.

    F   You will blink your eyes in the next 5 minutes.

2   Look at these cards.

    | 1 | 3 | 4 | 4 | 1 |

    Imagine taking a card without looking. Write 'true' or 'false' for each
    of these statements.

    a   I am equally likely to take a 1 or a 4.

    b   I have an even chance of taking a 4.

    c   I am more likely to take a 3 than a 5.

    d   I am less likely to take a 1 than a 3.

3   Gabriela is conducting a chance experiment by flipping a coin
    and recording whether it lands heads up or tails up.

    Gabriela says: 'I have flipped a head. My next flip must be a tail
    because there is an even chance of flipping a head or a tail
    and I have already flipped a head.'

    Is Gabriela correct? Explain your answer.

Probability tells us how likely something is to happen.

This machine holds 100 toys. The machine works by a player trying to control the claw to pick up a toy. If the player picks up a toy then they win it.

> How likely do you think it is for a player to win a toy?
>
> One of the toys is a small football. How likely do you think it is for a player to win the football toy?
>
> If you knew the likelihood of winning a toy how could that help you decide whether to play the game?

> 9.1 Describing and predicting likelihood

We are going to ...

- describe the chance of outcomes using the language of proportion and percentages

- learn about events that are mutually exclusive

- use likelihood to predict outcomes

- conduct probability experiments and describe the results.

If we can understand and describe the likelihood of different events occurring then we can predict how likely they are to occur in the future.

equally likely outcomes   event

mutually exclusive events

outcome   probability

probability experiment

We can use proportion and percentages to describe likelihood more precisely than words. What do you think the percentages on this weather forecast mean?

0600	0700	0800	0900	1000	1100	1200	1300	1400
13°	14°	15°	17°	18°	19°	20°	21°	21°
13%	15%	16%	15%	14%	16%	18%	20%	23%

1500	1600	1700	1800	1900	2000	2100	2200	2300
21°	21°	20°	20°	19°	17°	16°	15°	14°
26%	29%	31%	32%	32%	30%	26%	21%	16%

Is it likely or unlikely to rain? When is it most likely to rain? When is it least likely to rain?

Exercise 9.1

1   Zara puts one yellow ball, one red ball and two green balls in a bag. She takes one ball from the bag without looking.

a   The probability of a red ball being pulled from the

bag is _____ out of 4.

b   The probability of a yellow ball being pulled from

the bag is _____ out of 4.

c   The probability of a green ball being pulled from

the bag is _____ out of 4 or _____ %.

2 Write the probability of each of these events occurring as a percentage.

a taking a red card

b taking a 3

c taking a black card

d taking a card that is not a 3

3 Draw a set of cards for each description below.

a There is less than a 50% chance of taking an 8.

b The probability of taking a card with a value less than 5 is 5 out of 6.

c The chance of taking a 3 is greater than the chance of taking a 1.

d There is a greater than 50% chance of taking a 4.

e There is a 2 out of 5 chance of taking a 3.

> **Tip**
>
> Choose the number of cards for each description carefully. Check that it is possible to make the fraction, proportion or percentage in the description with the number of cards your have chosen.

4 Keran hears that the chance of a coin landing heads up is equally likely as the chance of it landing tails up. She does a probability experiment to see whether she will get the same number of heads up as tails up when she flips a coin multiple times.

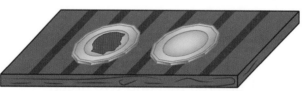

These are her results:

	Tally	Total
Heads up	⊦⊦⊦ ⊦⊦⊦ ⊦⊦⊦ ⊦⊦⊦ IIII	24
Tails up	⊦⊦⊦ ⊦⊦⊦ ⊦⊦⊦ I	16

a How many trials did Keran carry out?

b Does Keran's experiment show that the coin is more likely to land heads up or tails up?

c   What does Keran's experiment show is the experimental probability of the coin landing tails up?

d   Continue Keran's experiment. Record your outcomes in a table.

e   How many trials have you and Keran completed in total?

f   Including all the trials, what is the experimental probability of the coin landing tails up?

g   Ask your partner how they chose how many more trials to carry out in the experiment. Do they understand that larger numbers of trials are better for demonstrating the likelihood of an event than smaller numbers of trials?

Worked example 1

Which two of these events are mutually exclusive?

- Spin a 5.

- Spin a number greater than 2.

- Spin a number less than 4.

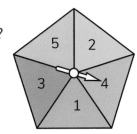

- Spin a 5.

- Spin a number greater than 2.

I could spin a 5, which would be both a 5 and greater than 2.

These events are not mutually exclusive.

- Spin a number greater than 2.

- Spin a number less than 4.

I could spin a 3, which would be both greater than 2 and less than 4.

These events are not mutually exclusive.

- Spin a 5.

- Spin a number less than 4.

I cannot spin a number that is both a 5 and less than 4.

These events are mutually exclusive.

Compare each of the events against each other.

Mutually exclusive means that the events cannot happen at the same time.

5 Some children play a game with tickets numbered from 1 to 30.
They take a ticket without looking. If their number is odd they win a
small prize. If their number is a multiple of 10 they win a medium prize.
If their number is both odd and a multiple of 10 then they win a big prize.

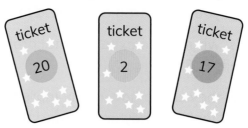

Copy and complete this Venn diagram with the numbers 1 to 30.

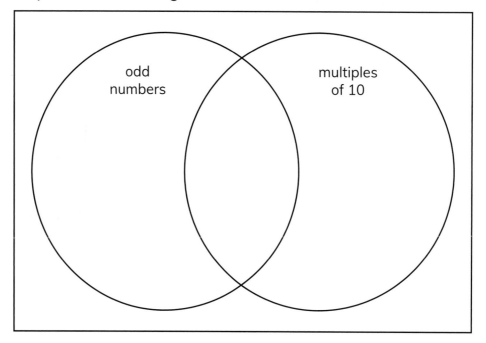

a   Colour the section of the diagram with the numbers that
would not win a prize in red.

b   Colour the section of the diagram with the numbers that
would win a small prize in blue.

c   Colour the section of the diagram with the numbers that
would win a medium prize in yellow.

d   What is the chance of winning a big prize? Why?

e   Are the events 'taking an odd number' and 'taking a multiple
of 10' mutually exclusive?

6   Look at the shapes in this bag.

Write 'mutually exclusive' or 'not mutually exclusive'
for these pairs of events for when **one** shape is taken
out of the bag.

a   Taking a shape that is red and blue.

b   Taking a shape that is red and a cone.

c   Taking a shape with more than 5 faces and is blue.

How confident do you feel about using the phrase
'mutually exclusive'? Could you write it in a sentence?
Could you use it in a conversation? Could you explain
what it means to someone who does not know?

7   You have two 1–6 dice. One is red and one is blue.

Imagine you are going to investigate these events:

Event A: You roll a double.

Event B: The sum of the two scores is even.

Event C: The score on the blue dice is greater than the score on the red dice.

Event D: You get a 6 on the red dice.

a   Which events can happen at the same time? Write 'yes' or 'no' for each one.

   i   A and B   ii   A and C   iii   A and D

   iv   B and C   v   B and D   vi   C and D

b   Which pairs of events are mutually exclusive?

c   Write two events of your own about the dice that are not mutually exclusive.

d   Write two events of your own about the dice that are mutually exclusive.

8   Look at this spinner.

Asubi uses his knowledge of likelihood and fractions to predict that after 8 spins the spinner is most likely to land on:

- red (★): 4 times

- blue (☺): 3 times

- yellow (✳): 1 time.

Predict how many times the spinner will land on each colour for these numbers of spins.

a   16 spins   b   40 spins   c   200 spins

Discuss with your partner how you predicted the number of times the spinner would land on each colour.

9   Take a total of 10 red and blue objects. For example, counters, cubes or beads.

a   How many blue objects did you take?

b   How many red objects did you take?

Hide the objects, for example, in a bag or under a cloth or piece of paper.

You are going to carry out an experiment to see if you can predict how many of each colour you will take. You are going to take, record and replace an object 20 times.

c   How many red objects would you expect to take? Why?

d   How many blue objects would you expect to take? Why?

e   Conduct the experiment. Record the colour of each counter you take in a tally chart.

f   Describe your results. Do your results match your prediction? If your prediction is different from your results, can you explain why?

Think like a mathematician

Vanessa makes this prediction:

There are 12 different outcomes when I roll two dice and add the numbers. The chance of rolling a 12 is one out of twelve. I predict that if I roll two dice 60 times I will most likely roll a 12 five times.

Vanessa draws this table to record her results.

Number rolled	Tally	Total
1		
2		
3		
4		
5		
6		
7		
8		
9		
10		
11		
12		

Work with a partner to complete Vanessa's investigation.

Talk about the investigation with your partner. Conjecture and discuss:

• Do you think Vanessa's prediction is a good prediction? Why?

• Is the result of your experiment what you expected? Why?

• What do you think would happen if you carried out more trials? Why?

Write about what you have discussed and found out.

Look what I can do!

☐ I can describe the chance of outcomes using proportion and percentages.

☐ I can say when two events are mutually exclusive.

☐ I can use likelihood to predict outcomes.

☐ I can conduct probability experiments and describe the results.

Check your progress

1 Describe the probability of these outcomes on the spinner.

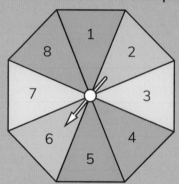

a The probability of the spinner landing on 8 is ☐ out of ☐ .

b The probability of the spinner landing on either 1 or 5 is ☐ out of ☐ .

c The probability of the spinner landing on a number greater than 7 is ☐ out of ☐ .

d The probability of the spinner landing on a number less than 3 is ☐ out of ☐ .

e The probability of the spinner landing on an even number is ☐ %.

f The probability of the spinner landing on a number that is not 1 or 5 is ☐ %.

2 Song was interested in these 3 events about the spinner in question 1.

Event 1: The spinner lands on 5.

Event 2: The spinner lands on a number less than 6.

Event 3: The spinner lands on a multiple of 3.

Which two of Song's events are mutually exclusive?

10 ▶ Multiplication and division (1)

Getting started

1 Calculate.

   a 704×6 b 34×27 c $603 \div 9$

2 Nine lamp posts are equally spaced along a river bank.

The posts are 180 metres apart. What is the distance between the first lamp post and the last lamp post in metres?

3 Find the missing digit.

$$\boxed{}\ \boxed{5}\ \boxed{2}\ \div\ \boxed{}\ \boxed{7}\ =\ \boxed{3}\ \boxed{6}$$

4 Zina is thinking of a multiple of 5 that is divisible by 8.

What is the smallest number Zina could be thinking of?

5 Here are four digit cards.

$$\boxed{0}\quad\boxed{1}\quad\boxed{2}\quad\boxed{3}$$

Use each card once to complete the calculation.

$$\boxed{}\ \boxed{}\ \times\ \boxed{}\ \boxed{}\ = 360$$

Lots of people multiply and divide numbers as part of their work.

Astronomer

Scientist

Teacher

Doctor

Can you think of other jobs where you need to multiply or divide?

This unit is all about multiplication and division.

> 10.1 Multiplication

We are going to ...

- estimate the size of an answer before calculating it
- multiply whole numbers up to 10 000 by 1-digit or 2-digit whole numbers.

product

Imagine you sell stamps.

Each sheet has 10 columns and 16 rows, and you have 12 sheets of stamps.

How many stamps do you have altogether?

You need to multiply 10 × 16 × 12 to find the answer.

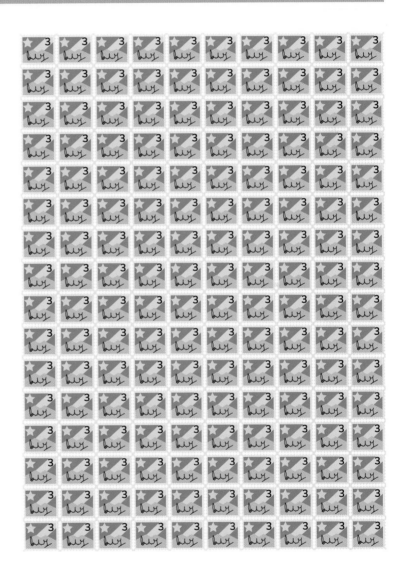

Can you think of times when you multiply numbers together?

Worked example 1

Find the product of 1347 × 8.

Estimate: 1000 × 8 = 8000	Start by making an estimate.
1500 × 8 = 12 000	The answer is between 8000 and 12 000.

```
    1 3 4 7
×         8
─────────────
          6
        5
```

7 × 8 = 56

Put 6 in the answer box and carry 5 tens.

```
    1 3 4 7
×         8
─────────────
        7 6
      3 5
```

40 × 8 = 320

Add 5 tens to give 37 tens. Put 7 tens in the answer box and carry 3 hundreds.

```
    1 3 4 7
×         8
─────────────
      7 7 6
    2 3 5
```

300 × 8 = 2400

Add 3 hundreds to give 27 hundreds. Put 7 hundreds in the answer box and carry 2 thousands.

```
    1 3 4 7
×         8
─────────────
  1 0 7 7 6
    2 3 5
```

1000 × 8 = 8000

Add 2 thousands to give 10 000.
Record in the answer box.

Answer:

10 776

Check your answer against the estimate to make sure it is reasonable.

Exercise 10.1

1   Lexi estimates the answer to 1499 × 59 to be 900 000.
    Has she made a good estimate? Explain your answer.

Tip

Remember to estimate all your answers before you do the calculation.

2   Calculate.

    a   4224 × 7   b   6174 × 6   c   3748 × 8

    Check your answers with your partner.

3   Find the product of 1234 and 7.

4   Pierre calculates 6024 × 7. His answer is not correct.

```
      6 0 2 4
  ×         7
  ─────────────
    4 2 8 6 8
  ─────────────
        1 2
```

Identify the error, then write the correct answer.

How did you decide what Pierre has done wrong?
How did you explain your answer? Did you think about
showing your answer on a diagram? This might be easier
than writing a sentence to explain your answer.

5   Which of these multiplications have the answer 24 000?

60 × 4000   400 × 60   80 × 3000

8000 × 3   20 × 1200

6   Kiki's heart beats about 79 times each minute. How many times
does her heart beat in a day?

7   Calculate.

   a   5489 × 30   b   3279 × 50   c   7621 × 70

8   Calculate.

   a   1356 × 19   b   1571 × 43   c   7625 × 57

Check your answers with your partner.

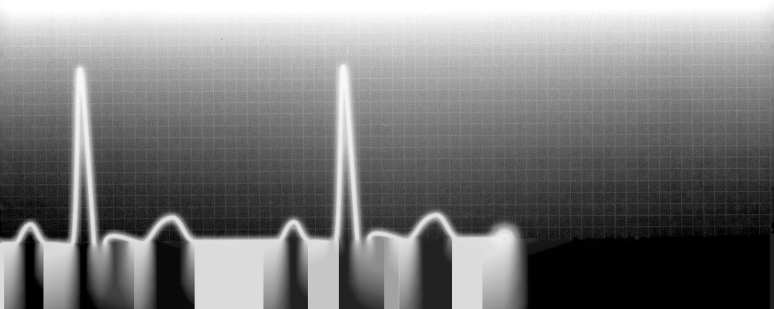

9 Each display cabinet has 7 shelves and each shelf holds 18 figures.
Joe has a collection of 25 cabinets and each cabinet is full.

How many figures are in Joe's collection?

Show your working.

10 Copy and complete this calculation by working out the three missing digits.

$$
\begin{array}{r}
3\ \square\ 2\ \square \\
\times\quad \square\ 2 \\
\hline
7\ 2\ 5\ 4 \\
1\ 4\ 5\ 0\ 8\ 0 \\
\hline
1\ 5\ 2\ 3\ 3\ 4 \\
\hline
\end{array}
$$

Think like a mathematician

Two consecutive numbers multiply together to make 650.

What are the two numbers?

Make up some more puzzles like this and swap them with a partner.

You will show you are **specialising** when you find the two numbers.

Tip

$20 \times 20 = 400$
and $30 \times 30 = 900$

Look what I can do!

☐ I can estimate the size of an answer before calculating it.

☐ I can multiply whole numbers up to 10 000 by 1-digit or 2-digit whole numbers.

> 10.2 Division

We are going to ...

- estimate the size of an answer before calculating it
- divide whole numbers up to 1000 by 1-digit whole numbers
- divide whole numbers up to 1000 by 2-digit whole numbers.

Three students are asked to estimate the answer to 936 ÷ 16

The answer is about 45 because 900 ÷ 20 is 45.

The answer is about 50 because 1000 ÷ 20 is 50.

The answer is about 60 because 900 ÷ 15 = 60.

Which estimate would you use? Why?

In this section you will learn how to divide larger numbers. It is important to make an estimate so you can check your answer is reasonable.

dividend   divisor
quotient   remainder

Worked example 2

Calculate 552 ÷ 24.

Estimate: 600 ÷ 25 = 24 so the answer will be close to 24.

```
        2 3
    _____
24 ) 5 5 2
   – 4 8 0        24 × 20
    _____
     7 2
    – 7 2         24 × 3
    _____
       0
```

Answer: 23

Start with an estimate by rounding the dividend and the divisor. Round 552 to 600 and 24 to 25 then 600 ÷ 25 = 14.

There are twenty 24s in five hundred and fifty-two. Record 2 tens on the answer line. Subtract 480 (24 × 20) from 552 to leave 72.

There are three 24s in seventy-two. Record 3 ones on the answer line. Subtract 72 (24 × 3) from 72 to leave 0.

Compare your answer with the estimate to check that it is reasonable.

Exercise 10.2

1   Pablo estimates the answer to all these calculations is 30.

$598 ÷ 21$ $914 ÷ 34$ $564 ÷ 14$ $342 ÷ 13$

Do you agree? Explain your answer.

2   a   Calculate 765 ÷ 7.

    b   Divide 297 by 11.

    c   Divide 308 by 11.

Check your answers with your partner. Did you show your working in the same way?

3   Parveen and Ingrid both calculate 493 divided by 7.

Parveen says, 'The answer is 70 remainder 3.'

Ingrid says, 'The answer is $70\frac{3}{7}$.'

Who is correct? Explain your answer.

4   Here are two calculation cards A and B.

$$A = 588 \div 14$$ $$B = 374 \div 11$$

What is the difference between A and B?

5   Use factors to work out these calculations.

a $924 \div 12$ b $960 \div 15$ c $882 \div 18$

Check your answers with your partner.

6   Eggs are put in boxes. Each box holds 12 eggs.

A farmer has 684 eggs. How many boxes does he need to pack his eggs?

 7   Mandy says, 'I can work out $825 \div 15$ by dividing by 10 and then dividing by 5.'

Do you agree with Mandy? Explain your answer.

 8   Use the numbers from the circles to copy and complete the two number sentences.

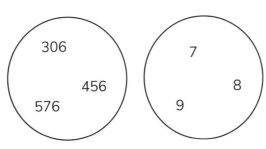

306
456
576

7
8
9

$\boxed{}\ \boxed{}\ \boxed{} \div 72 = \boxed{}$

$\boxed{}\ \boxed{}\ \boxed{} \div 34 = \boxed{}$

9   a   Find the missing digits.

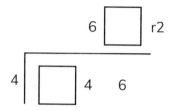

b   Write the answer as a mixed number

10 A meal in a restaurant costs the same for each person.

For 11 people the meal costs $297. What is the cost for each person?

11 Work out the value of the missing digit.

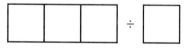

a   39 ▢ ÷ 6 = 65 remainder 3

b   76 ▢ ÷ 9 = 84 remainder 8

Think about the methods you used to answer these questions. Did your partner choose the same methods? Which methods were the most efficient? Did you remember to estimate and check?

Think like a mathematician

Choose any four digits.

Arrange them to make a division calculation:

▢▢▢ ÷ ▢

Work out the answer.

Try other arrangements using the same four digits.

- Which arrangement gives the largest answer?

- Which arrangement gives the smallest answer?

You will show you are **specialising** when you find solutions to the problem.

Look what I can do!
☐ I can estimate the size of an answer before calculating it.
☐ I can divide whole numbers up to 1000 by 1-digit whole numbers.
☐ I can divide whole numbers up to 1000 by 2-digit whole numbers.

〉 10.3 Tests of divisibility

We are going to ...
• learn and use tests of divisibility for 3, 6 and 9.

divisible	divisibility test	factor
multiple	Venn diagram	

Can you share the cookies so that you and five of your friends all get the same number?

Divisibility tests for whole numbers are useful because they help you quickly find out if a number can be divided without leaving a remainder.

Worked example 3

Write a digit in the box so the number is divisible by 3.

Can you find more than one answer?

80 ☐ 17

---

8 + 0 + 1 + 7 = 16   Find the sum of the digits used.

Answer: The sum of the digits must be a multiple of 3,
80 217 or 80 517 or 80 817   so you can add 2 or 5 or 8.

143 〉

Exercise 10.3

1   Which of these numbers is divisible by 3? Explain how you know.

   935   9203   43 719

   Check your answers with your partner.

2   Find the missing digits to copy and complete the calculations.

   a | 1 | | × 3 = | 5 | 7 |

   b | | | × 3 = | 5 | 1 |

   c | | | × 3 = | 4 | |

3   Jiao is thinking of a number. She says, 'My number is between 50 and 100. It is divisible by 3 and 4. The tens digit is double the ones digit.'

   What number is Jiao thinking of?

4   Start at 99 and list the next four numbers that are divisible by 9.

5   Find a number between 90 and 100 that is divisible by 6.

 6   Copy the Venn diagram.

   Put these numbers on the diagram.

   16   21   24   27   36

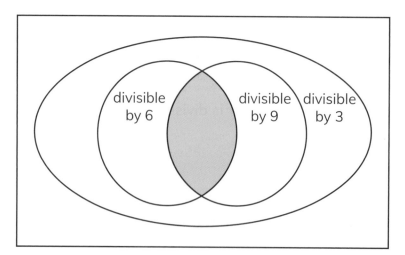

   What do you know about the numbers in the yellow region?

7   Copy the table. Put ticks in the boxes to show whether these numbers are divisible by 3, 6 and 9.

	Divisible by 3	Divisible by 6	Divisible by 9
987			
495			
3594			

8   Oscar is thinking of a number. He says, 'My number is between 200 and 220. It is divisible by 6. The sum of the digits is 3.'

What number is Oscar thinking of?

9   Write a digit in each box so that all the numbers are divisible by 3.

a   23 ▢   b   3 ▢ 5   c   83 ▢ 49

Can you find more than one answer to this question?
If you were asked to find all the possible answers, what would you do?

Think like a mathematician

Paulo has forgotten the 4-digit number that allows him to unlock his case. He knows that the number:

- is less than 3000
- is divisible by 3
- has a tens digit that is divisible by 3
- has a hundreds digit that is divisible by 3
- has a ones digit that is bigger than the tens digit
- has a ones digit and a thousands digit that are not multiples of 3
- has no zeros.

Find all the numbers that satisfy all these conditions.

You will show you are **specialising** when you find numbers that satisfy the criteria.

Look what I can do!

☐ I know and can use tests of divisibility for 3, 6 and 9.

Check your progress

1 Calculate.

    a 3459×8 **b** 7846×30 **c** 7542×34

    d $539 \div 7$ **e** $648 \div 12$ **f** $969 \div 51$

2 Is it always, sometimes or never true that an even number that is divisible by 3 is also divisible by 6?

3 Jamila says, 'I can check my calculation using the inverse operation.' Use Jamila's method to check these calculations:

    a $23 \times 4 = 92$ **b** $117 \div 9 = 14$

    Record your results.

4 Vijay and Kofi complete the same multiplication.

Vijay

2	3	4	5
	×		4
9	2	8	0

  1   1   2

Kofi

2	3	4	5
	×		4
9	3	8	0

  1   1   2

Who has the correct answer?

What mistake has the other child made?

5 A chef bakes apple pies.

She has 15 boxes of apples. Each box holds 16 apples.

She uses 3 apples for each pie. How many pies can she make?

11 ▶ 3D shapes

Getting started

1 Match each of these shapes to its correct drawing on isometric paper.

A 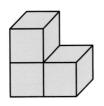 B 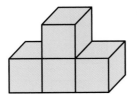 C 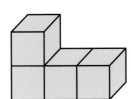 D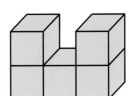

i

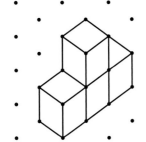

ii

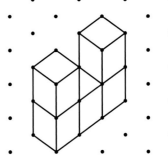

iii

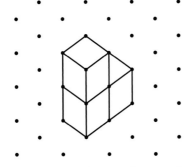

iv

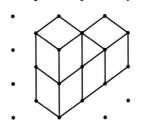

Continued

2   Li draws these nets on squared paper.

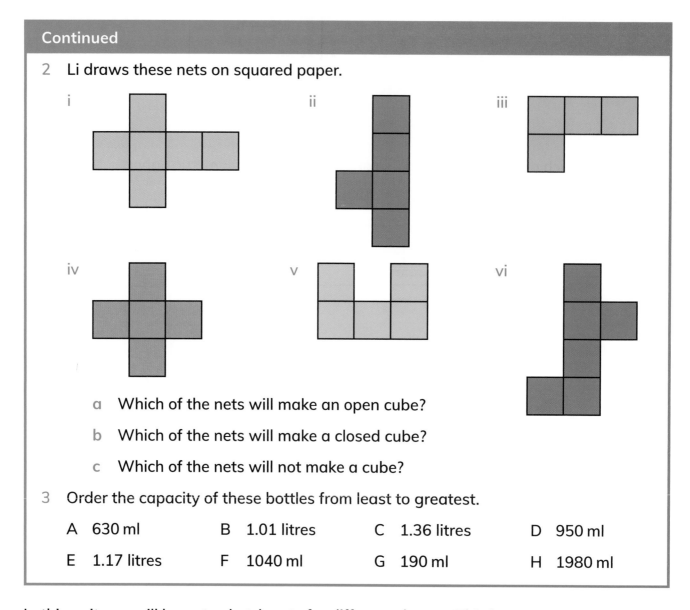

i

ii

iii

iv

v

vi

   a   Which of the nets will make an open cube?

   b   Which of the nets will make a closed cube?

   c   Which of the nets will not make a cube?

3   Order the capacity of these bottles from least to greatest.

   A   630 ml   B   1.01 litres   C   1.36 litres   D   950 ml

   E   1.17 litres   F   1040 ml   G   190 ml   H   1980 ml

In this unit you will learn to sketch nets for different shapes. This is a really important skill if you are designing gift boxes to hold things such as chocolates, toys or jewellery.

> 11.1 Shapes and nets

We are going to ...

- identify, describe and sketch compound 3D shapes

- identify and sketch different nets for cubes, cuboids, prisms and pyramids

- look at the relationship between area of 2D shapes and surface area of 3D shapes.

When you see a person delivering a parcel to someone, what is the usual shape of the box? You will probably say a cuboid, but it is possible to have boxes that are cubes, pyramids or prisms as well. If you are working in a factory that makes the boxes, you need to know what to do to make the different shape boxes!

compound shape
prism   surface area

Worked example 1

Describe this compound shape.

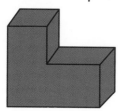

This compound shape is either:	Think how you can split the compound shape into simpler 3D shapes that you know.
a cube and a cuboid	
OR	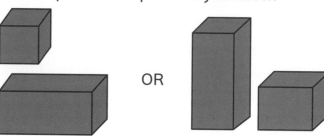
two cuboids	

Exercise 11.1

1 Describe these compound shapes.

a

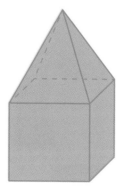

b

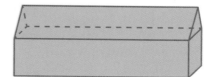

c

2   Classify these shapes into two groups.

- Group 1: simple shapes
- Group 2: compound shapes

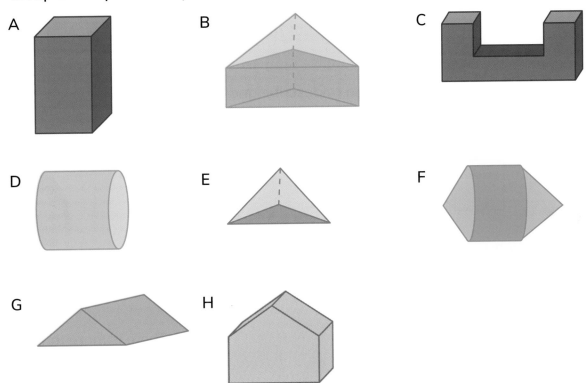

3   Sketch a compound shape that is made from these simple shapes.

a   two different cuboids

b   a cuboid and a square-based pyramid

c   two different cylinders

4 This is part of Deema's homework.

Question: Describe and sketch a net of this cuboid.

Solution: A cuboid has six faces.

In this cuboid four of the faces are rectangles and two are squares.

Use the same method as Deema to describe and sketch a net of these shapes.

a cube

b square-based pyramid

c cylinder

d triangular-based pyramid

Tip

There is more than one net for each of these shapes but you only need to sketch one of them.

Think like a mathematician 1

a Marcus asks this question:

'How do you work out the surface area of a cuboid?'

What do you think Marcus means by the surface area of a cuboid? How do you think he could work it out?

b How could you work out the surface area of

i a cube   ii a square-based pyramid?

c Copy and complete this general rule:

The surface area of a 3D shape is the total area of all its _____ .

d Discuss your answers to parts a to c with other learners in your class.

5   This diagram shows a triangular prism.

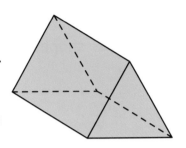

   a   Copy and complete this description of the triangular prism.

      A triangular prism has a total of _____ faces.

      Two of the faces are _____ and _____ of the faces
      are rectangles.

   b   Sketch a net for the triangular prism.

6   Match each of these shapes to the correct net.

   A   pentagonal prism   B   octagonal prism   C   hexagonal prism

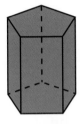   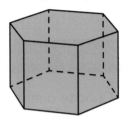

   i   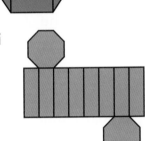   ii   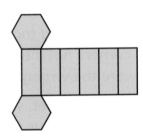   iii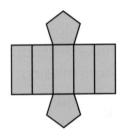

Think like a mathematician 2

This shape is made of unit cubes.

   a   What is the smallest number of unit cubes that must
      be added to the shape to make a cuboid?

   b   Write down the method that you used to work out
      the answer to part **a**.

   c   Discuss your method with other learners in your class.
      Critique each other's methods. Can you now improve
      on your method?

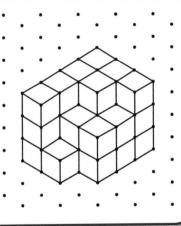

7   Write down the smallest number of unit cubes that must be added
    to these shapes to make cuboids.

a   b   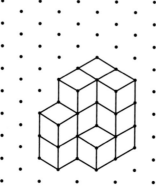   c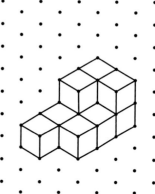

Think like a mathematician 3

a   Choose a simple 3D shape and draw a net for that shape on a piece of paper.

b   Cut the net out, using a pair of scissors, and fold your net to make the shape.

c   What do you think of your net? Did it fold together accurately to
    make the shape or did some corners not meet? Did you have any
    faces missing, or faces that were the wrong shape?

d   Give yourself a score out of 10 for your net, with 1 being not very good and 10
    being perfect. How could you improve your score if you made the net again?

e   Discuss your answers to parts c and d with a partner.

Look what I can do!

☐   I can identify, describe and sketch compound 3D shapes.

☐   I can identify and sketch different nets for cubes, cuboids,
    prisms and pyramids.

☐   I can understand the relationship between area of 2D shapes and
    surface area of 3D shapes.

> 11.2 Capacity and volume

We are going to ...

- look at the difference between capacity and volume.

When you are cooking or baking you need to measure out ingredients. Solid ingredients such as rice, pasta or vegetables can be weighed on kitchen scales. When you measure liquid ingredients such as milk, oil or water you will need to use a measuring jug.

capacity

volume

If you want the perfect pancakes, you need to measure the correct amount of milk!

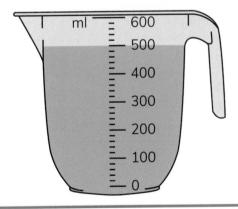

Worked example 2

The diagram shows some water in a jug.

a   What is the capacity of the jug?

b   What is the volume of water in the jug?

| a | 600 ml | 600 ml is the <u>maximum</u> the jug can hold. |
| b | 500 ml | The scale shows the water is at the 500 ml mark. |

Exercise 11.2

1   For each of these jugs write down:

    i   the capacity of the jug   ii   the volume of water in the jug.

a    b 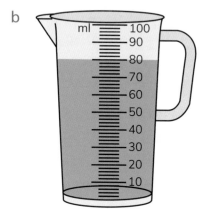   c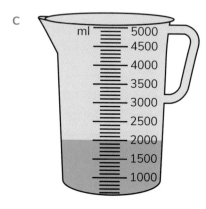

2   Read what Sofia says.

You can write a volume of 2500 ml as 2 litres 500 ml or 2.5 litres.

Tip

Use the fact that 1 litre = 1000 ml to help you explain.

    a   Give a convincing reason to justify why Sofia is correct.

    b   Use Sofia's example to help you copy and complete this table.

millilitres	litres and millilitres	litres
2500 ml	2 litres 500 ml	2.5 l
3200 ml		
	4 litres 300 ml	
		3.7 l
	0 litres 800 ml	
12 100 ml		

Think like a mathematician 1

Marcus and Arun are looking at this question:

What is the volume of water in this jug?

Read their conjectures.

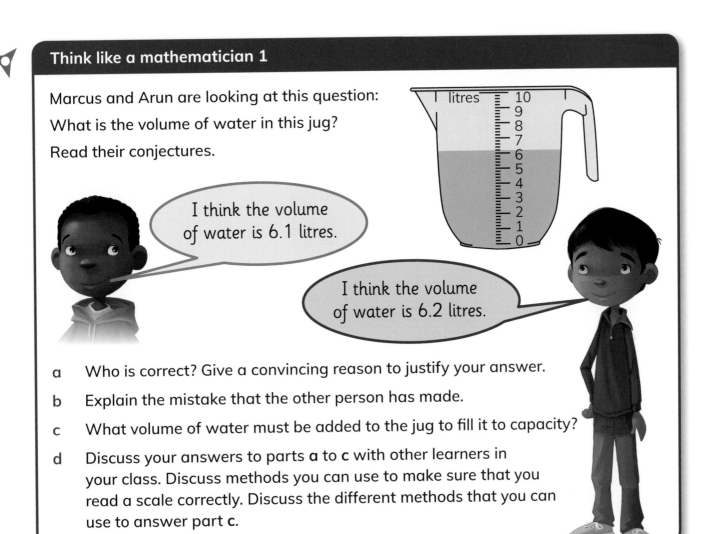

I think the volume of water is 6.1 litres.

I think the volume of water is 6.2 litres.

a   Who is correct? Give a convincing reason to justify your answer.

b   Explain the mistake that the other person has made.

c   What volume of water must be added to the jug to fill it to capacity?

d   Discuss your answers to parts **a** to **c** with other learners in your class. Discuss methods you can use to make sure that you read a scale correctly. Discuss the different methods that you can use to answer part **c**.

3   For each of these jugs write down:

   i   the capacity of the jug

   ii   the volume of water in the jug.

4   What volume of water must be added to these jugs to fill them to capacity?

a

b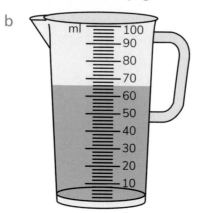

c

5   Chipo needs to measure out 2.3 litres of milk.

She only has the measuring jug shown.

Explain how she can use this measuring

jug to measure out 2.3 litres of milk.

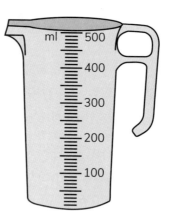

6   Vishan buys a fish tank with a capacity of 120 litres.

He pours water into the tank until it is $\frac{3}{4}$ full.

What is the volume of the water in the tank?

Think like a mathematician 2

Work with a partner to answer this question.

Mair has these four measuring cups, A, B, C and D.

The capacity of each cup, in millilitres, is shown.

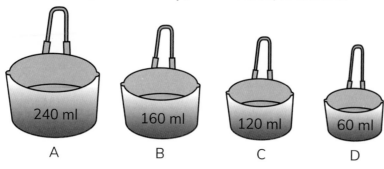

Continued

a   Give a convincing explanation to show how Mair can use the cups to accurately measure out these volumes:

    i   400 ml   ii   360 ml

    iii   420 ml   iv   320 ml

    v   180 ml   vi   600 ml

b   Discuss your answers to part **a** with other learners in your class.

> **Tip**
>
> I think that if Mair wanted to accurately measure out 300 ml of water, she could fill cup A and cup D.

7   Each of these containers (A–F) is marked with its capacity.
Estimate the volume of liquid in each container.

A 1 litre   B 800 ml   C 3 litres   D 1800 ml

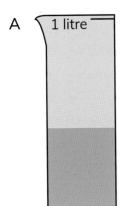   

E 1.5 litres   F 2 litres

> **Tip**
>
> Estimate what fraction of the container is full. Work out that fraction in millilitres or litres.

Order the volumes of liquid from the least to the greatest.

8 Copy and complete the Carroll diagram to sort the containers by their capacity and the volume of liquid they contain.

	Volume of 500 ml or less	Volume of more than 500 ml
Capacity of 1 litre or less		
Capacity of more than 1 litre		

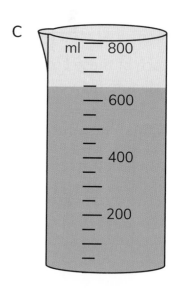

A
ml — 1200
— 1000
— 800
— 600
— 400
— 200

B
ml — 2000
— 1500
— 1000
— 500

C
ml — 800
— 600
— 400
— 200

D
litres — 1.5
— 1.25
— 1
— 0.75
— 0.5
— 0.25

E
ml — 200
— 180
— 160
— 140
— 120
— 100
— 80
— 60
— 40
— 20

F
litres — 0.9
— 0.8
— 0.7
— 0.6
— 0.5
— 0.4
— 0.3
— 0.2
— 0.1

Think like a mathematician 3

a   Jug A has a capacity of 3 litres. Jug B has a capacity of 4 litres. Investigate what amounts you can make with jug A and jug B when neither jug has a measurement scale.

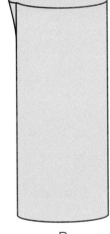

The combined capacity of the two jugs is 7 litres. You can make a volume of any whole number of litres, from 1 litre to 7 litres. You can fill a whole jug, pour water from one jug to the other or empty a jug.

Investigate and record how each volume can be made.

A   B

b   Investigate which amounts of whole litres can be made with a 3 litre jug (A) and a 5 litre jug (B).

c   Predict what amounts you will be able to make with 3 litre (A) and 6 litre (B) jugs.

Check your prediction and record which numbers of whole litres can be made and how they are made.

Suggest an explanation for what you have found out.

d   Choose two jugs of your own to investigate. Make sure each jug is a different size. Predict what volumes can be made. Investigate your problem, record your results and check your prediction. Write what you have found out.

Look back at the questions in this exercise.
Which ones have you found the easiest and which ones have you found the hardest?
Do you feel confident in answering all the different types of question?
What can you do to increase your level of confidence?

Look what I can do!

☐   I can understand the difference between capacity and volume.

Check your progress

1 Describe these compound shapes.

a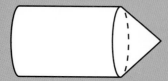

b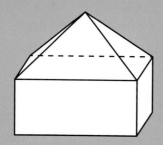

c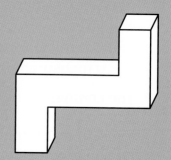

2 Sketch a compound shape that is made from a cuboid and a triangular prism.

3 This diagram shows a square-based pyramid.

a Copy and complete this description of the square-based pyramid.

A square-based pyramid has a total of _____ faces. Four of the faces are _____ and _____ of the faces is a square. The surface area of a square-based pyramid is the total area of all its _____ .

b Sketch a net for the square-based pyramid.

4 Write down the smallest number of unit cubes that must be added to this shape to make a cuboid.

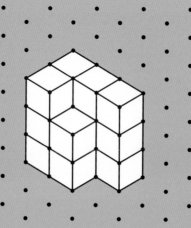

Continued

5 The diagram shows a jug containing water.

a Write down

   i   the capacity of the jug

   ii the volume of water in the jug.

b What volume of water must be added to the jug to fill it to capacity?

12 ⟩ Ratio and proportion

Getting started

1   A bag contains striped, plain and spotty counters.

Copy and complete these sentences.

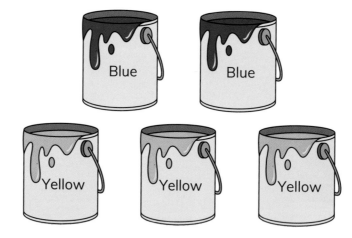

a   The ratio of striped to plain counters is _____ .

b   The proportion of striped counters is _____ .

c   The ratio of spotty to plain to striped counters
    is _____ .

2   Bao is mixing paint.

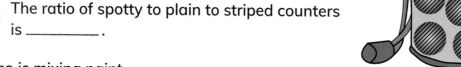

She uses 2 cans of blue paint and 3 cans of yellow paint to make green paint.

Write whether each statement is true or false.
Correct any statements that are false.

a   The ratio of yellow to blue in green paint is 2 : 3.

b $\frac{2}{5}$ of green paint is blue.

c   60% of green paint is yellow.

d   2 in every 3 parts of green paint is blue.

Continued

3   Odette says, 'My diagram shows that 1 out of every 3 shapes is a triangle.'

Explain why Odette might think she is correct.
What should she have written?

In this unit, you will learn about equivalent ratios and direct proportion.

When two quantities are in direct proportion their ratio stays the same.
Here are some examples.

Recipes

You decide to make chocolate chip cookies for the maths club.

You need 120 grams of butter to make 10 cookies.

How much butter do you need to make 20 cookies?

Work pay

Kate is a builder.

The more hours she works, the more money she earns.

Hours worked	Money earned
1	$20
2	$40
3	$60
4	$80

Can you think of any other examples of direct proportion?

> 12.1 Ratio

We are going to ...

- find and use equivalent ratios
- find a ratio in its simplest form.

A ratio is a relationship between two or more numbers.

| equivalent ratio   ratio |
| simplest form (ratio) |

This bowl of fruit contains six apples and three oranges.

The ratio of apples to oranges is six to three.

We write this as 6 : 3 and this is equivalent to 2 : 1.

In this unit, you will learn about equivalent ratios.

Worked example 1

In a survey, the ratio of people who preferred apples to bananas was 3 : 5.
45 people preferred bananas.

How many people took part in the survey?

3 : 5 = ☐ : 45 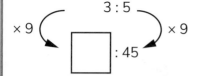	You need to find an equivalent ratio where the number for bananas is 45.
	Multiply both sides of the ratio by 9 because 5 × 9 = 45.
3 : 5 is equivalent to 27 : 45	27 people preferred apples and 45 people preferred bananas.

Answer:

Total number of people = 27 + 45 = 72

Exercise 12.1

1 Look at these shapes.

Write in its simplest form:

a   the ratio of circles to squares

b   the ratio of squares to pentagons

c   the ratio of pentagons to squares.

2 Write these ratios in their simplest form.

a   3 : 12   b   21 : 14   c   12 : 9

d   24 : 8   e   150 : 25   f   15 : 300

> How do you know when you have found a ratio in its simplest
> form? Think about the work you did on simplifying fractions.
> What are the similarities between the two tasks?

3 Write the missing numbers.

a   2 : 3   b   5 : 7   c   3 : 5

12 : ☐   ☐ : 21   15 : ☐

Check your answers to question 3 with your partner.

 4 Place the ratios in the correct position in the table.
One ratio cannot be placed. Which one is it?

18 : 27   12 : 16   28 : 35   16 : 20   4 : 6   14 : 21   24 : 32

18 : 24   36 : 27   36 : 45   21 : 28   8 : 12   32 : 40

Equivalent to 2 : 3	Equivalent to 3 : 4	Equivalent to 4 : 5

5 Pierre plants 4 carrots for every 3 onions. He plants 48 carrots.

   a How many onions does he plant?

   b How many carrots and onions does he plant altogether?

6 The ratio of girls to boys in a dance competition is 3 : 2.

   42 girls take part in the competition.

   How many boys and girls take part in the competition altogether?

7 Ollie and Igor share 24 counters in different ways.

   a How many counters does Igor get when he has twice as many as Ollie?

   b How many counters does Igor get when he has one counter for every three counters Ollie has?

   c Igor and Ollie share the counters in the ratio 3 : 5. How many counters does Igor get?

Think like a mathematician

Marcus spent $4 on beads to make necklaces.

White beads cost 10 cents each and coloured beads cost 20 cents each.

Marcus bought beads in the ratio of white to coloured = 3 : 1.

How many white and coloured beads did he buy?

Tip

Try tabulating your information. For example:

Number of white beads	Cost of white beads	Number of coloured beads	Cost of coloured beads	Total cost

You will show you are **specialising** when you find solutions to the problem.

You will show you are **classifying** when you tabulate your information.

Look what I can do!

☐   I can find and use equivalent ratios.

☐   I can find a ratio in its simplest form.

❯ 12.2 Direct proportion

We are going to ...

- learn what 'in proportion' means

- learn that when one quantity increases (or decreases) the other quantities increase (or decrease) in the same ratio.

direct proportion
proportion

Have you ever taken a photograph and liked it so much that you wanted a bigger copy to put on your wall or a smaller copy to stick in a notebook?

In mathematics we call these larger and smaller versions enlargements. The lengths of lines in the photo and the enlargement are in proportion and all the angles stay the same size.

In this section, you will learn about shapes and objects that are in proportion.

Worked example 2

Dakarai cooks pasta and pasta sauce.

Pasta sauce

300 g tomatoes
120 g onions
75 g mushrooms

a   Dakarai needs 350 grams of pasta for 4 people.

   How much pasta does he need for 12 people?

b   The recipe for pasta sauce is for 6 people.

   How many grams of tomatoes does Dakarai need for 12 people?

a $4 \times 3 = 12$	To get from 4 people to 12 people you multiply by 3.
$350 \times 3 = 1050$ grams	So multiply 350 by 3 to find the mass of pasta.
b $6 \times 2 = 12$	To get from 6 people to 12 people you multiply by 2.
$300 \times 2 = 600$ grams	So multiply 300 by 2 to find the mass of tomatoes.

Exercise 12.2

1   3 melons cost $2. What is the cost of 15 melons?

2   Magda organises a meal for 12 people. She buys 1 pizza for every 3 people.
   How many pizzas does Magda buy?

3 Here is a recipe for ice cream.

Raspberry ice cream

[for 8 people]

400 ml cream

500 ml milk

1 kg raspberries

250 g sugar

Kiki makes ice cream for 4 people. Write a list of the ingredients she uses.

4 A teacher buys 24 posters for his classroom. He can buy 4 posters for $7. How much does the teacher spend on posters?

5 The length of a model car is one-tenth the size of the real car.

a The model car is 40 cm long. What is the length of the real car?

b The real car is 150 cm high. How tall is the model car?

c A wheel on the model car has diameter 4.25 cm.
What is the diameter of a wheel on the real car?

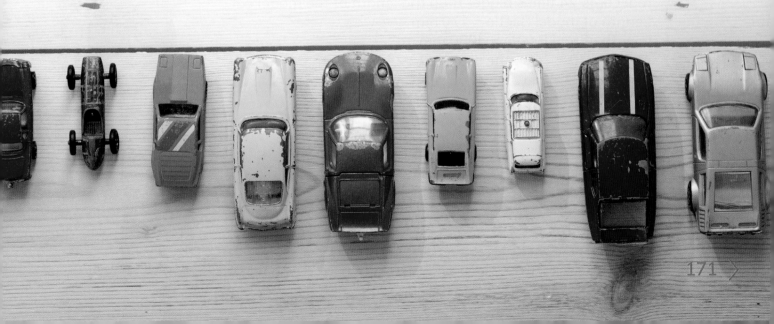

6 You will need a calculator for this question.

Dimitri has five model cars. He knows they are built to a scale of 1 : 18 or 1 : 24 or 1 : 32 but he does not know which scale has been used for each car.

He measures the length of the model cars:

Beetle 170 mm   **Puma** 230 mm

Delta 140 mm   **Embla** 190 mm   **Modi** 160 mm

This table shows the lengths of the real cars.

Car	Beetle	Puma	Delta	Embla	Modi
Length in mm	4080	4140	4480	4560	5120

Work out the scale used for each car and copy and complete the sorting diagram.

Scale 1 : 18	Scale 1 : 24	Scale 1 : 32

Tip

Remember that a scale of 1 : 24 means that the length of the real car is 24 times bigger than the length of the model car.
Length of model Beetle = 170 mm
Length of real Beetle = 4080 mm
4080 ÷ 170 = 24 so the scale is 1 : 24.

7   Here is rectangle A.

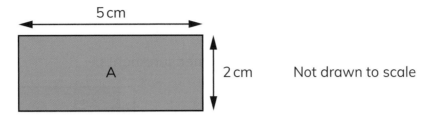

5 cm

A

2 cm   Not drawn to scale

Rectangle A is enlarged to make rectangles B, C and D.

- The length of each side of rectangle B is twice the corresponding length of rectangle A.

- The length of each side of rectangle C is four times the corresponding length of rectangle A.

- The length of each side of rectangle D is six times the corresponding length of rectangle A.

Copy and complete the table.

	Ratio of rectangle sizes	Length in cm	Width in cm	Perimeter in cm
A		5	2	
B	A to B = 1 : 2	10		
C	A to C = 1 : 4			
D	A to D = 1 : 6			

Check your answers with your partner.

What have you learned in this unit? Think of one thing you need to do to improve your work.

Think like a mathematician

Paper sizes

Look at this table of paper sizes and their measurements.

Size	Width × height (mm)
A0	841 × 1189
A1	594 × 841
A2	420 × 594
A3	297 × 420
A4	210 × 297
A5	148 × 210

What do you notice about the measurements?

What is the height of A6 paper?

For each paper size, try dividing height by width.
You can use a calculator.
What do you notice about your results?

You will show you are **generalising** when you notice something about your results.

If you ask yourself questions based on your observations, you will show you are **conjecturing**.

Look what I can do!

☐ I know what in proportion means.

☐ I know that when one quantity increases (or decreases) the other quantities increase (or decrease) in the same ratio.

Check your progress

1 Write these ratios in their simplest form.

    a 9 : 12   **b** 7 : 21   **c** 3 : 15   **d** 24 : 6

2 At the running club there are 2 boys for every 3 girls.

    a There are 12 girls at the club. How many boys are there?

    b On a different day, there are 12 boys at the club.
       How many girls are there?

3 Here is a recipe for a fruit smoothie.

Fruit smoothie

[makes 2 smoothies]

2 mangoes

$\frac{1}{2}$ litre apple juice

250 ml yogurt

1 banana

Write the quantities needed for 4 smoothies.

4 Here is rectangle A.

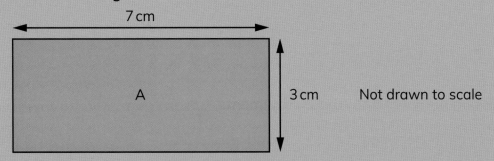

7 cm

A

3 cm   Not drawn to scale

Rectangle B is in proportion to rectangle A but every length in B is
5 times the length in A.

What is the perimeter of rectangle B?

Getting started

1   Cards **A**, **B**, **C** and **D** describe part of a turn. Cards **i**, **ii**, **iii** and **iv** show a number of degrees. Match each card **A** to **D** with its correct card **i** to **iv**.

| **A** full turn | **B** half turn | **C** quarter turn | **D** three-quarter turn |

    i   90°   **ii**   270°   **iii**   360°   **iv**   180°

2   State whether each of these angles is acute, right, obtuse, reflex.

a
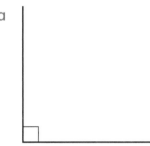

b
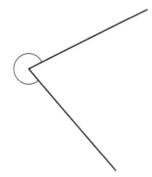

c
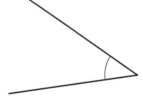

d

3   Write the missing numbers from these statements.

   a   An acute angle is between _____° and _____°.

   b   A reflex angle is between _____° and _____°.

   c   An obtuse angle is between _____° and _____°.

Continued

4   Calculate the size of the lettered angles in these diagrams.

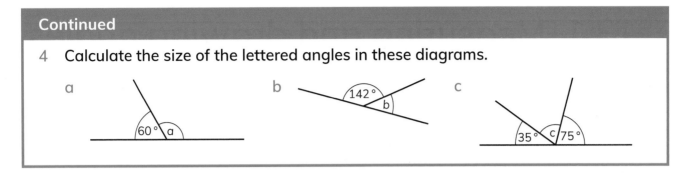

a

b

c

There are many people who measure and draw angles as part of their jobs.

An architect is a person who designs buildings. When they draw a plan of a building, they need to measure and draw the angles for the roof, the staircases and the walls.

The measurements need to be very accurate. If they are not accurate, the builder may find that the roof isn't big enough to cover the building, the staircases don't reach high enough and there are gaps between the walls!

> 13.1 Measuring and drawing angles

We are going to ...

- measure angles
- draw angles.

When you measure and draw straight lines, you need to use a ruler.
When you measure and draw angles, you need to use a protractor.

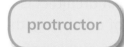

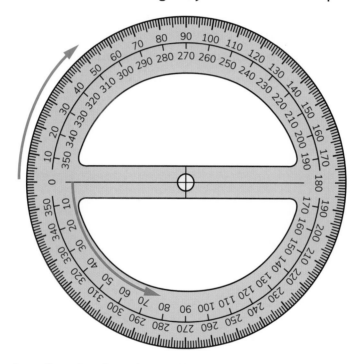

A protractor is a flat circular object that has 0 ° to 360 ° marked around
its edge. It is usually made of plastic so you can see through it.
When you measure clockwise from 0 ° you use the numbers on the
outside circle. When you measure anticlockwise from 0 ° you use the
numbers on the inside circle.

You can use a letter to represent the size of an angle. In the diagram
on the right you can work out the size of angle x by measuring the
angle with a protractor.

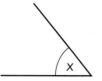

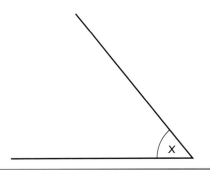

Worked example 1

a   Estimate and then measure the size of angle x.

b   Draw an angle of 120°.

Note: the protractors in this worked example
are not to scale.

a

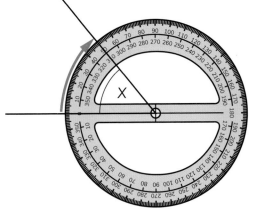

Estimate: x = 45° Accurate: x = 50°

Write down an estimate of
the angle first, then measure
it using your protractor.
Place your protractor over
angle x so that the centre of
your protractor is at the point of your
angle. Make sure the horizontal arm of
your angle is lined up exactly with 0°.
As the angle opens clockwise, use the
numbers on the outside circle.

b

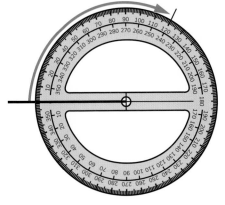

Start by drawing a horizontal line.
Place the centre of your protractor on
the right end of the line, with the left
end of the line at 0°. Measure 120°
clockwise, using the outside numbers.
Mark a small line as this point.

c

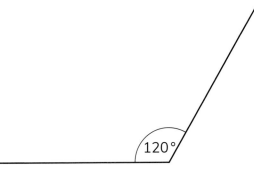

120°

Now take away the protractor and
join your mark to the right end of the
horizontal line. Draw an angle arc and
write 120° onto your diagram.

Exercise 13.1

1   Estimate and then measure the size of each of these acute angles.

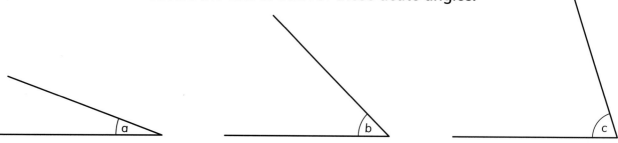

2   Estimate and then measure the size of each of these obtuse angles.

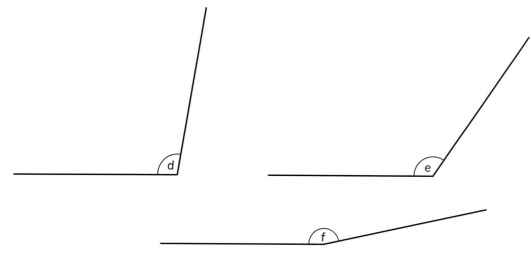

3   Estimate and then measure the size of each of these reflex angles.

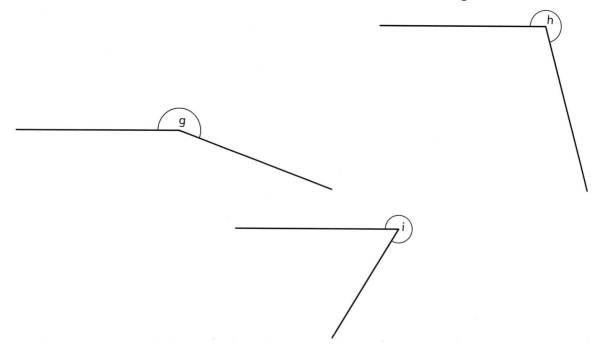

Think like a mathematician

Work with a partner.

The diagrams show two angles x and y.

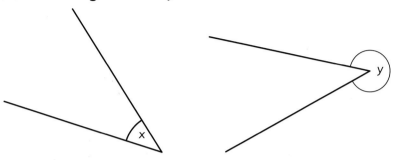

Find as many different ways as you can to use your protractor to measure the size of the angles.

Discuss your methods with other learners in your class.

4 a Draw angles of the following sizes.

i 30° ii 145° iii 245° iv 350°

b In your book, write down three different angles of your choice between 0° and 360°. On a piece of paper accurately draw these angles, but do not write the sizes of the angles on them.

c Swap your piece of paper with a partner. Measure the angles that they have drawn. Check your answers with their answers. Did you measure each other's angles correctly? Discuss any mistakes that were made.

5 The diagram shows angles x and y.

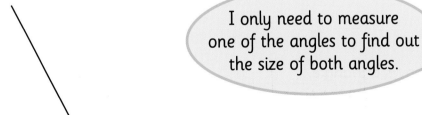

I only need to measure one of the angles to find out the size of both angles.

a Is Sofia correct? Give a convincing reason to justify your answer.

b Write down the sizes of angles x and y. Explain the methods you used to find them.

6 a Measure the size of angles v and w in this diagram.

b Explain the calculation you can do to check that
your answers to part **a** are correct.

7 An architect is designing a building.

The diagram shows a wheelchair
ramp for the building.

For a wheelchair ramp to be allowed,
the size of the angle of the ramp, r, must
be <u>no more than</u> 20 °.

a Is this wheelchair ramp allowed?
Use specialising to explain your answer.

b The best wheelchair ramps have
an angle of between 7 ° and 15 °.
Draw an example of one of these
ramps. Make sure you write the
angle you have used on your diagram.

8 The diagram shows angles x, y and
z on a straight line.

a Measure and write down the sizes
of angles x, y and z.

b Show how to check your answers
to part **a** are correct.

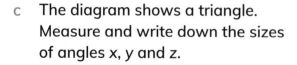

c The diagram shows a triangle.
Measure and write down the sizes
of angles x, y and z.

d What do you notice about your answers
to parts **a** and **c**?
Discuss and compare your conjectures
with other learners in your class.

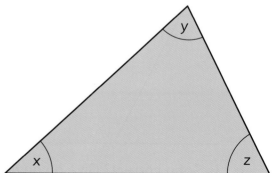

a   What have you found hardest, measuring or drawing angles? How do you think you can improve?
b   Write down three important points that you must remember when using a protractor.

Look what I can do!

☐   I can measure angles.

☐   I can draw angles.

> 13.2 Angles in a triangle

We are going to ...

- find the sum of the angles in a triangle

- use the sum of the angles in a triangle to work out missing angles.

Think like a mathematician

On a piece of paper, draw a triangle. It can be a triangle of any size, but make sure you use a ruler to draw the sides. Mark the angles with arcs.

Now carefully cut out your triangle using scissors.

In your book, draw a straight horizontal line. Gently tear the angles off your triangle, and put them, points together along the straight line you have drawn.

What do you notice?

What can you say about the sum of the angles in a triangle?

Worked example 2

Work out the size of angle x in this triangle.

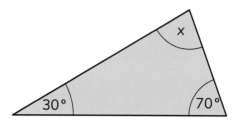

equilateral triangle
isosceles triangle
scalene triangle

30° + 70° = 100°	Add together the two angles that you know.
180° − 100° = 80°	The angles in a triangle add to 180°, so subtract the total so far from 180°.
x = 80°	Write down the value of x.

Exercise 13.2

1 Work out the size of angle x in each of these triangles.

a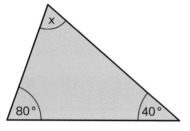

b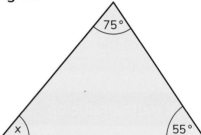

c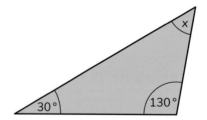

2 Work out the size of angle y in each of these triangles.

a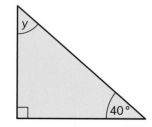

b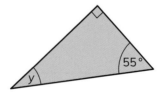

Tip

The symbol └ means a right angle (90°).

3   This is part of Felipe's homework. His homework is correct.

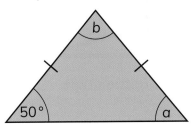

Tip

Remember that an isosceles triangle has two equal sides and two equal angles.

Question: This triangle is isosceles. Work out the size of angles *a* and *b*.

Solution: $a = 50°$

$180° - 50° = 130°$

$130° - 50° = 80°$

$b = 80°$

a   How did Felipe know that $a = 50°$?

b   Critique Felipe's solution. Is it easy to follow?
    Explain your answer.

c   Can you think of a way to improve Felipe's solution?

d   Discuss your answers to parts **a** and **b** with other learners in
    your class. Which do you think is the best solution and why?

4   Work out the size of angle *z* in each of these triangles.

a

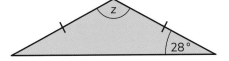

b

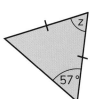

Tip

Remember that the two lines \ and / show which sides are equal.

5   Show that the size of angle *m* in this triangle is 27°.

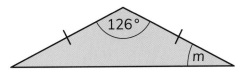

6   The diagram shows the roof of Alice's house.

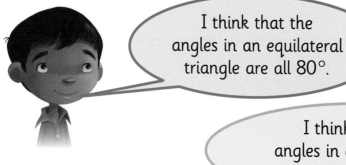

She wants to put some special tiles on her roof, but the angle marked p needs to be at least 15 °.

Can she use the special tiles? Explain your answer.

7   Arun and Marcus work out the size of the angles in an equilateral triangle. Read their conjectures.

> I think that the angles in an equilateral triangle are all 80°.

> I think that the angles in an equilateral triangle are all 60°.

a   Who is correct?

b   Show that the person you chose in part **a** is correct and that the other one is incorrect.

8   The cards show the sizes of two of the angles of triangles A to I.

| Triangle A
35°, 45° | Triangle B
55°, 55° | Triangle C
100°, 40° |

Tip

You may have to work out the size of the third angle in each triangle.

| Triangle D
60°, 60° | Triangle E
90°, 30° | Triangle F
48°, 52° |

| Triangle G
90°, 45° | Triangle H
36°, 106° | Triangle I
60°, 60° |

a   Classify these triangles into groups.

Describe the characteristics of each group.

Tip

The different types of triangles are scalene, isosceles, equilateral and right-angled.

b   Which is the only triangle that is a right-angled isosceles triangle?

 9   The diagram shows a triangle on a straight line.

84°

b

a   127°

a   Which of these rules can you use to work out the size of angle a?

| Angles in a triangle add up to 180°. |

| Two of the angles in an isosceles triangle are the same size. |

| All of the angles in an equilateral triangle are the same size. |

| There are 360° in a full turn. |

| There are 90° in a right angle. |

| Angles on a straight line add up to 180°. |

b   Work out the size of angle a.

c   Work out the size of angle b.
Which rule did you use to work out the size of angle b?

Check your progress

1   Measure the size of each of these angles.

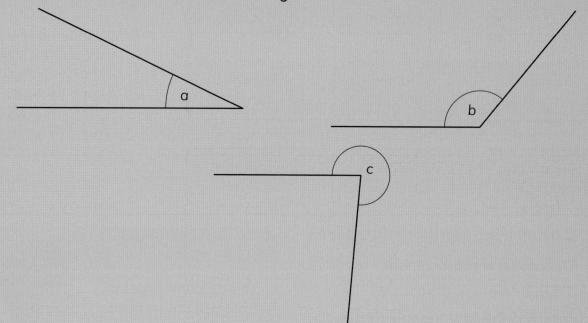

2   Draw angles of the following sizes.

   a   80°   b   175°   c   315°

3   Work out the size of angle x in each of these triangles.

   a 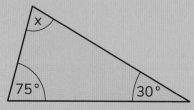   b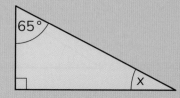

4   Work out the size of angle y in each of these triangles.

   a

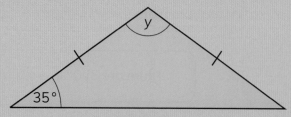

   b

> Project 5

Animal angles

In a field, a photographer is taking pictures of some animal homes – a tree, a pond, a bird's nest and a spider's web. She sets the camera up on a tripod, pointing it at the tree.

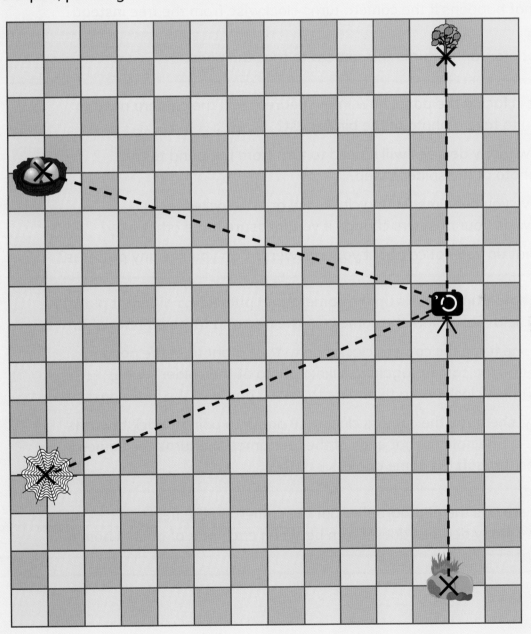

Continued

How many degrees anticlockwise will the camera need to turn from the tree to take a photo of the bird's nest?

How many degrees anticlockwise will it need to turn from the tree to take a photo of the spider's web?

What happens if the camera turns clockwise from the tree instead?

The photographer turns the camera to face the pond.

If it is facing the pond, how many degrees will the camera need to turn to take a photo of the bird's nest?

How many degrees will it need to turn from the pond to take a photo of the spider's web?

Have you been measuring clockwise or anticlockwise?
How do your answers change if you measure it the other way?

What do you notice about your answers? Can you see any patterns?

The photographer picks up the camera and puts it in a different place in the field. She points the camera at the tree and takes a photo of it.

Then she turns the camera clockwise to take a photo of the pond. She turns the camera again to take a photo of the spider's web, and turns it clockwise a third time to take a photo of the bird's nest.

Finally, she turns the camera clockwise again to point it back towards the tree. She notices that each of the four times she turns the camera, it turns through the same angle.

Where has the photographer put the camera in the field?
How many degrees does it turn between each pair of animal homes?

14 ▶ Multiplication and division (2)

Getting started

1 Here are six numbers.

    6   7   8   21   24   40

Use each number once to copy and complete these statements.

a $\frac{1}{3}$ of ☐ = ☐   b $\frac{1}{4}$ of ☐ = ☐   c $\frac{1}{5}$ of ☐ = ☐

2 Lan spilled ink on his work. What are the digits covered by the ink?

a $0.7 \times 9 = 6.$ ●   b $0.9 \times 5 = $ ●$.5$ c $0.$ ●$\times 8 = 4.8$

3 Find the product of 4567 and 8.

4 9 friends share $315 equally. How much does each friend receive?

Here are some examples of how we use fractions and decimals in our everyday lives. Can you think of some more?

You go out to eat with your friends and family. The waitress brings one bill that you share between you.

You save up to buy a new pair of trainers. Your parent agrees to pay half the cost.

You have half a cake to divide equally between four friends.

In this unit you will learn more about multiplying and dividing fractions and decimals.

> 14.1 Multiplying and dividing fractions

We are going to ...

- multiply a proper fraction by a whole number
- divide a proper fraction by a whole number.

Mia cut $\frac{1}{4}$ of a pizza for her dad. She shared the rest of the pizza into four equal pieces for her brothers and sisters. What fraction of the pizza did each child get?

Mia is dividing a fraction by a whole number.

In this unit you will learn about multiplying and dividing fractions by a whole number.

> denominator   numerator   operator
> proper fraction   unit fraction

Worked example 1

Calculate $\frac{2}{3} \div 4$

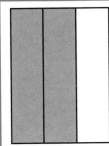 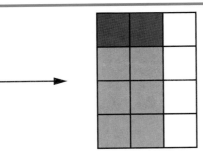

$\frac{2}{3} \div 4 = \frac{2}{12}$

$= \frac{1}{6}$

Draw a diagram to show $\frac{2}{3}$.

Divide each third into 4 equal parts.

The dark grey section represents $\frac{2}{3} \div 4$.

This is 2 parts out of 12 equal parts which is $\frac{2}{12}$.

The fraction can be simplified to $\frac{1}{6}$.

Exercise 14.1

1   Write an addition sentence **and** a multiplication sentence for the total of the shaded parts of this diagram.

2   Write a multiplication sentence that is equivalent to this addition diagram.

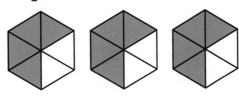

$+\frac{2}{8}$ $+\frac{2}{8}$ $+\frac{2}{8}$ $+\frac{2}{8}$ $+\frac{2}{8}$

0

3   Calculate.

a $\frac{3}{5} \times 2$ b $\frac{7}{8} \times 5$ c $\frac{5}{6} \times 4$

Check your answers with your partner.

Tip

Remember to change improper fractions to mixed numbers. Estimate your answer before working it out, so you know the size of the answer you should get.

4   Copy the sorting table and write the letter of each expression in the
    correct place.

A $\dfrac{2}{8} \times 4$ B $3 \times \dfrac{2}{3}$ C $\dfrac{3}{4} \times 4$ D $\dfrac{2}{8}$ of 4

E $\dfrac{2}{3} \times 3$ F $\dfrac{2}{8} + \dfrac{2}{8} + \dfrac{2}{8} + \dfrac{2}{8}$ G $\dfrac{3}{4} + \dfrac{3}{4} + \dfrac{3}{4} + \dfrac{3}{4}$ H $\dfrac{2}{3}$ of 3

Answer = 1	Answer = 2	Answer = 3

5   Saif writes the calculation $5 \times \dfrac{2}{3}$.

    Which of the following statements is true?

    A   The answer is between 1 and 2.

    B   The answer is between 2 and 3.

    C   The answer is between 3 and 4.

    D   The answer is between 4 and 5.

6   Oscar, Bruno and Ali equally share $\dfrac{2}{3}$ of a large pie.

    What fraction of the whole pie did each boy get?
    Draw a diagram to show your answer.

7   Calculate.

a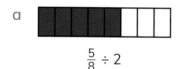

$\dfrac{5}{8} \div 2$

b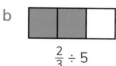

$\dfrac{2}{3} \div 5$

8   Calculate.

a $\dfrac{4}{5} \div 2$ b $\dfrac{5}{8} \div 2$ c $\dfrac{3}{5} \div 5$

Check your answers with your partner.

9   Write a whole number less than
    10 in each box to make these
    number sentences correct.

a $\dfrac{2}{3} \div \boxed{} = \dfrac{1}{9}$ b $\dfrac{3}{4} \div \boxed{} = \dfrac{1}{12}$

> **Tip**
>
> Remember that dividing by 2 is the same
> as multiplying by $\dfrac{1}{2}$, dividing by 3 is the
> same as multiplying by $\dfrac{1}{3}$ and so on.

You can write improper fractions as mixed numbers and you can write some fractions in a simper form.
In this exercise, how did you decide whether you could write your answer in a different way?

Think like a mathematician

Find values that make this number sentence correct.

$$\underset{\text{fraction}}{\boxed{}} \div \underset{\text{whole number}}{\boxed{}} = \frac{5}{24}$$

You will show you are **specialising** when you find values to make the number sentence correct.

Look what I can do!

☐ I can multiply a proper fraction by a whole number.

☐ I can divide a proper fraction by a whole number.

> 14.2 Multiplying decimals

We are going to ...

- estimate then multiply numbers with up to 2 decimal places by a 1-digit whole number

- estimate then multiply numbers with up to 2 decimal places by a 2-digit whole number.

Erik works in a theatre selling tickets.

Erik sells 63 tickets. Each ticket costs $45.75.

In this section, you will learn how to calculate the total cost of all the tickets Erik sells.

decimal number   decimal place
decimal point   product

Worked example 2

Calculate $\$45.75 \times 63$.

Estimate $50 \times 60 = 3000$

		4	5 .	7	5
	×	6	3		
	1	3	7 .	2	5
2	7	4	5 .	0	0
2	8	8	2 .	2	5
		1			

45.75×3

45.75×60

Always start with an estimate. You can round both numbers and then multiply them together to give a rough answer.

Multiply 45.75 by 3

Multiply 45.75 by 60

These stages can be done in either order.

Add the two answers together.

Check the answer is close to your estimate of 3000.

Answer: $\$2882.25$

Exercise 14.2

1 Calculate.

   a 45.1×5 b 38.12×7 c 40.09×9

   Check your answers with your partner.

2 Find the product of 6 and 34.56.

3 Vincent is thinking of a number.

   He says, 'If I divide my number by 6 the answer is 17.54.'

   What number is Vincent thinking of?

4 Calculate.

   a 74.36×15 b 95.36×47 c 23.08×83

   Check your answers with your partner.

> **Tip**
>
> Always remember to estimate before you calculate.

5 Parveen calculates 17.05 × 15

		1	7 .	0	5
	×	1	5		
		8	5 .	7	5
	1	7	0 .	5	0
	2	5	6 .	2	5
	1		1		

She has made an error.

Explain why her answer is not correct.

What advice would you give Parveen to help her avoid similar errors?

6 Use the digits 5, 6 and 7 to make this calculation correct.

$$\boxed{}\,.\,\boxed{4}\,\boxed{} \times \boxed{}\,\boxed{} = 32.35$$

7 Meals cost $15.25 at a restaurant.

12 people go for a meal.

What is the total cost of the meals?

8 Ravi and Tara buy some stickers.

Ravi buys 36 stickers at $0.98 each.

Tara buys 3 packs of 12 stickers for $11.50 a pack.

How much more does Ravi pay than Tara?

Think about how you worked out the answers.
Did you remember to estimate and check?
Did your partner use the same method?
Which method do you think is the most efficient?

Think like a mathematician

You need five cards.

| 2 | 3 | 4 | 5 | 6 |

Arrange the cards as a multiplication calculation.

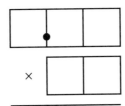

Investigate different answers. You can use a calculator.

Which calculation gives an answer closest to 208?

You will show you are **specialising** when you find solutions to the problem.

Look what I can do!

☐ I can estimate then multiply numbers with up to 2 decimal places by a 1-digit whole number.

☐ I can estimate then multiply numbers with up to 2 decimal places by a 2-digit whole number.

> # 14.3 Dividing decimals

We are going to ...

• estimate then divide a number with 1 or 2 decimal places by a 1-digit whole number

• estimate then divide a number with 1 or 2 decimal places by a 2-digit whole number.

Mandisa wants to know which of these packs contains the cheaper oranges.
Which pack should she choose?

dividend   divisor   quotient

Pack A	Pack B
4 oranges for $2.50	3 oranges for $1.89

To find the answer, Mandisa must divide the cost by the number of oranges.

In this section, you will learn how to divide decimals by whole numbers.

Worked example 3

Calculate $55.2 \div 24$.

Estimate: $50 \div 25 = 2$ so the answer will be a little more than 2.

$$
\begin{array}{r}
2.3 \\
24 \overline{)55.2} \\
-48.0 \quad 24 \times 2 \\
\hline
7.2 \\
-7.2 \quad 24 \times 0.3 \\
\hline
0
\end{array}
$$

or use a more compact way of recording:

$$
\begin{array}{r}
2.3 \\
24 \overline{)55\,5.^72}
\end{array}
$$

Answer: $55.2 \div 24 = 2.3$

Round 55.2 to 50 and 24 to 25 which is a factor of 50. We have rounded 55.2 down and 24 up, so the accurate answer will be greater than the estimated value.

There are two 24s in 55.2. Record 2 ones on the answer line. Subtract 48.0 from 55.2 to leave 7.2.

7.2 divided by 24 is 0.3 (because $72 \div 24 = 3$). Record 3 in the tenths position on the answer line.

Subtract 7.2 from 7.2 to leave 0.

Exercise 14.3

1   Calculate.

   a $37.2 \div 4$ b $3.2 \div 8$ c $0.36 \div 4$ d $140.05 \div 5$

   Check your answers with your partner.

2   Calculate.

   a $36.84 \div 12$ b $75.75 \div 15$

   Check your answers with your partner.

3   Find the missing digit.

$$12\overline{)\square 6.4}^{\,7.2}$$

4   Ahmed is thinking of a number.

   He multiplies his number by 14 and the answer is 86.8.

   What number is Ahmed thinking of?

5   Find the odd one out.

   $7.75 \div 5$ $9.3 \div 6$ $12.32 \div 8$ $13.95 \div 9$

   Explain your answer.

6   Ella, Kiki and Mandy spend $29.52 on food.

   They share the cost equally between them.

   How much does Mandy pay?

7   Two shops sell the same paint.

   Shop A sells 4 pots of paint for $6.88.

   Shop B sells 3 pots of paint for $5.22.

   Which shop has the better deal? Explain your answer.

8   A regular pentagon is drawn on the playground.

   The perimeter of the pentagon is 26.25 metres.

   What is the length of one side of the pentagon?

Tip

Always remember to estimate before you calculate.

Tip

For question 3, think about the answer to 7 × 12.

In Unit 10, you divided whole numbers by 1- and 2-digit numbers. Think about how you have applied the knowledge and skills you learned to work in this unit.

Think like a mathematician

Use each of the digits 2, 3, 4, 5 and 6 to complete this calculation. You can use a calculator.

329.68 ÷ ☐☐ = ☐·☐☐

> **Tip**
>
> Use the fact that $300 \div 50 = 6$ as a starting point.

You will show you are **specialising** when you find solutions to the problem.

Look what I can do!

☐ I can estimate then divide a number with 1 or 2 decimal places by a 1-digit whole number.

☐ I can estimate then divide a number with 1 or 2 decimal places by a 2-digit whole number.

Check your progress

1 Calculate.

   a $3 \times \frac{4}{5}$ b $\frac{5}{6} \times 7$ c $9 \times \frac{2}{3}$

2 Calculate $\frac{2}{3} \div 5$ and $\frac{2}{5} \div 3$.

   What do you notice about your answers?

3 Sally pays $0.35 for each minute she uses her phone.

   She spends 15 minutes talking to her friend.

   How much does the call cost?

4 Find the odd one out.

   $36.75 \div 21$ $8.6 \div 5$ $10.5 \div 6$ $19.25 \div 11$

   Explain your answer.

5 Multiply each whole number by each fraction.

   6   8   10 $\frac{7}{8}$ $\frac{3}{4}$ $\frac{5}{8}$

   a What is the smallest answer?

   b What is the largest answer?

15 ▶ Data

1 Ali kept a record of the weather for 30 days. Here are the results:

Cloudy, cloudy, rainy, rainy, cloudy, rainy, cloudy, cloudy, sunny, cloudy, cloudy, sunny, sunny, cloudy, sunny, sunny, sunny, cloudy, sunny, sunny, sunny, cloudy, cloudy, sunny, cloudy, cloudy, cloudy, rainy, rainy, rainy.

   a   Draw and complete a tally chart of the data.

   b   Represent the data in a waffle diagram with 30 squares.
       Don't forget to include a key.

2 Two groups of children were asked how long it took them to travel to school. The results are represented in these frequency diagrams.

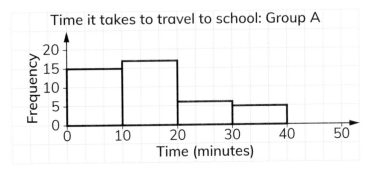

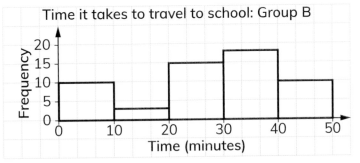

Tip

If the measurement is on the group boundary then it is recorded in the group above. For example, on this graph a travel time of 30 minutes is put in the group 30 to 40 minutes.

Continued

a   What is the most common amount of time it takes children in Group A to get to school?

b   How many children in Group B take between 10 and 20 minutes to get to school?

c   How many children in Group A take less than 20 minutes to get to school?

d   More children in Group B take longer to get to school than the children in Group A. Give a possible explanation for the difference between the two groups' times to get to school.

When you represent data using charts, graphs or diagrams it makes it easier to notice patterns in the data and it becomes clearer to share and communicate the information.

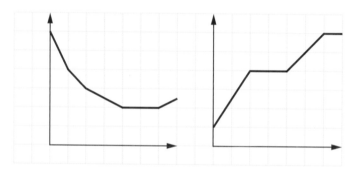

Describe the patterns you can see the in the graphs.
Suggest what each graph could be about and give them a title.
What would the axes labels be for the graphs?

> 15.1 Bar charts, dot plots, waffle diagrams and pie charts

We are going to ...

- interpret and represent data in bar charts, dot plots, waffle diagrams and pie charts

- plan and carry out investigations using data in categories and with whole numbers

- predict the outcome of an investigation, look for patterns and check predictions.

The data in this section are all whole numbers or can be put into categories. We can represent this kind of data using bar charts, pictograms, waffle diagrams and pie charts.

> bar chart   data   dot plot
> pie chart   waffle diagram

Exercise 15.1

1   This dot plot shows how many marks children scored in a test.

   a   How many children scored 7 marks?

   b   How many children scored more than 5 marks?

   c   How many children took the test?

   d   What is the highest score that children scored on the test?

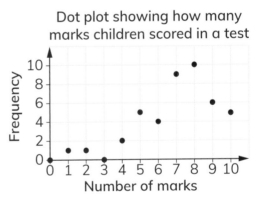

Dot plot showing how many marks children scored in a test

2   Ken and Ben record how many goals they score for the school hockey team in each match they play.
These dot plots show the results.

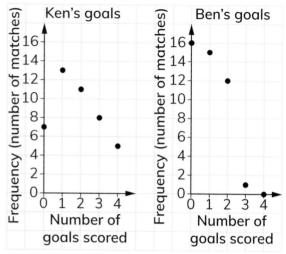

a   In how many games did Ken score 2 goals?

b   In how many games did Ben score 2 goals?

c   How many matches did each player play?

d   Give a possible explanation for the differences in the numbers of goals Ken and Ben scored.

3   This bar chart shows the number of roses in bloom on the rose bushes in a park.

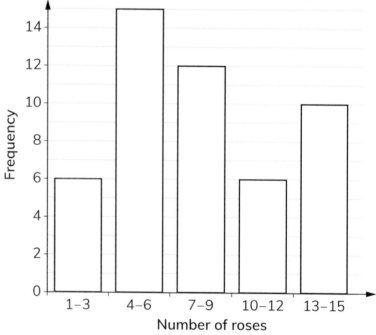

A bar chart showing the number of roses in bloom on all the rose bushes in the park

a   Which group shows the most common numbers of roses in bloom on the bushes?

b   Which group has the least common number of roses in bloom?

c   How many bushes have the range 7 to 9 roses in bloom?

d   How many bushes have the range 13 to 15 roses in bloom?

e   How many more bushes are in the range 4 to 6 than 1 to 3?

f   How many more bushes are in the range 13 to 15 than 10 to 12?

g   How many bushes were looked at in total in the park?

4   A farmer carried out a survey to find out how many peas grew in the pea pods.

These are the peas found in the pods that were surveyed:

4, 8, 12, 5, 9, 7, 15, 11, 13, 8, 5, 18, 14, 12, 7, 3, 8, 9, 17,

13, 6, 14, 10, 8, 5, 4, 13, 10, 11, 20, 15, 14, 12, 15, 12, 9,

7, 18, 15, 16, 4, 9, 7, 12, 15, 13, 7, 4, 7, 9, 13, 10, 11, 13,

6, 9, 10, 13, 7, 8, 13, 12, 10, 14, 8, 5, 7, 4, 11, 14, 12, 10.

a   What was the highest number of peas found in one pod?

b   Choose a sensible group size and draw a tally chart to record the number of pods in each group.

c   Draw a bar chart to represent the information.

d   Describe one thing that the farmer could have found out from this data.

5   A group of 20 children each chose their favourite sport.
Their choices are represented in this 100 square waffle diagram.

A waffle diagram showing the favourite sports of 20 children

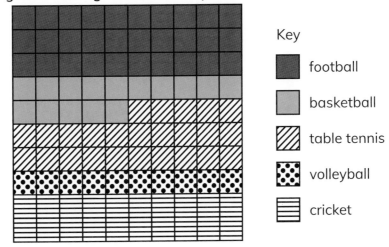

Key

■ football

□ basketball

▨ table tennis

▩ volleyball

▤ cricket

a   What was the most popular sport?

b   What was the least popular sport?

c   What percentage of the children chose table tennis?

d   How many children chose table tennis?

e   What percentage of the children did not choose football?

f   How many children did not choose football?

6 A different group of 20 children chose these sports.

a Copy and complete the table.

Sport	Frequency	Percentage
Football	5	
Basketball	9	
Table tennis	3	
Volleyball		5%
Cricket	2	

b Draw a 100 square waffle diagram to show the proportion of each sport chosen by this group of children.
Don't forget to include a key and a title.

c If you were organising a sporting event for both groups to take part in together, which sport would you choose?
Be convincing and explain your choice using the data from questions **5** and **6**.

d Read your partner's choice and explanation for part **c**.
Assess whether they use the data accurately to make a convincing argument.

Worked example 1

Zara wants to find out her cousins' favourite animals. She represents the data in the table in a pie chart.

Favourite animal	Frequency
Elephant	1
Tiger	2
Giraffe	2

1 + 2 + 2 = 5

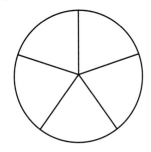

Find the total frequency.

Draw a circle and divide it into 5 equal sections. This is an empty pie chart.

Key

 Elephant

 Tiger

 Giraffe

My cousins' favourite animals

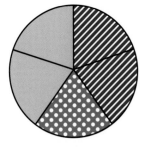

Choose three colours, one for each animal. Draw a key.

Add a title to show what the data represents.

Colour the sections of the pie chart according to the key and the table.

My cousins' favourite animals

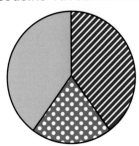

The lines within coloured sections do not need to be visible.

7   Two groups of art students chose their favourite tool for drawing.

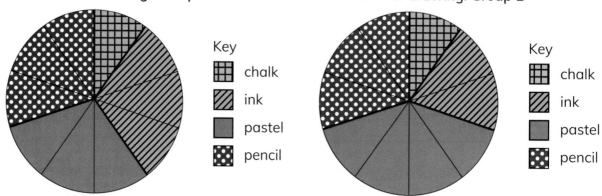

A pie chart showing art students' favourite tool for drawing: Group A

A pie chart showing art students' favourite tool for drawing: Group B

Key
chalk
ink
pastel
pencil

a   What fraction of Group B preferred to draw with:

   i   ink   ii   pastel   iii   pencil?

b   What percentage of Group B preferred to draw with:

   i   chalk   ii   ink   iii   pastel?

c   Use the information from the pie charts to characterise and describe a way that the preferences of the two groups are similar.

d   Use the information in the pie charts to characterise and describe a way that the preferences of the two groups are different.

8   Asif asked his friends how they travelled to school. He drew this frequency table of their answers.

Draw a pie chart to represent the data in the table.
Don't forget to add a key and a title.

Type of transport	Frequency
Walk	5
Car	1
Bus	3
Cycle	1

9   Choose the graph or chart that would be best to represent data for each of these investigations.

   a   You want to show whether any candidate received more than 50% of the vote in an election. Would you use a dot plot or a pie chart? Why?

   b   You want to show which candidate got the most votes in an election. Would you use a bar chart or a waffle diagram? Why?

10 Work in a group or with your whole class to think of a problem you can investigate by asking a question to each person in your class. For example, you might want to know what music to play at a class party and so ask everyone a statistical question about their favourite music groups.

   Work together to answer these questions, and collect and analyse the data.

   a   What is our question?

   b   How will we collect the data?

   c   What do we predict the data will show? Why?

   d   How will we represent our data? Why?

   e   Represent the data in our chosen graphs, charts and diagrams.

   f   What does the data show?

   g   Does the data answer our question?

   h   Was our prediction correct? How can we tell?

   i   Are there any other data that we could collect to find out more?

   Discuss as a group or a class what you did at each step of the data handling cycle and what you found out.

11 Suggest what problem might be investigated by each of these statistical questions:

   a   Which sport is most popular in our class?

   b   What are the most common shoe sizes in our classroom right now?

   c   How many of each different plant is growing in the school grounds?

   d   What proportion of people in our class is left-handed?

Think like a mathematician

Investigate your own problem where the data will be whole numbers or categories.

You could use one of the questions in question **11** to investigate a problem.

Ask your teacher to check your question before you start investigating.

Write a sentence explaining what you think will be the result of your investigation and why.

Collect your data in a frequency table.

Choose two ways to represent your data. You could choose a bar chart, dot plot, waffle diagram or pie chart. Explain why you chose those two ways of representing your data.

Describe any patterns you can see in your data.

Does your data suggest that your prediction was correct?

Use the information in your table, graph and charts to answer your statistical question.

Look what I can do!

- ☐ I can interpret and represent data in bar charts, dot plots, waffle diagrams and pie charts.

- ☐ I can plan and carry out investigations using data in categories and with whole numbers.

- ☐ I can predict the outcome of an investigation, look for patterns and check predictions.

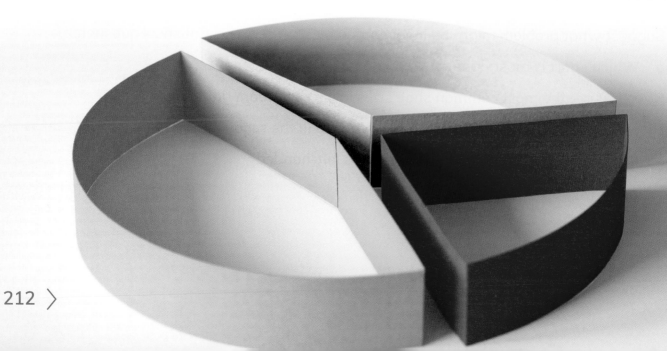

> 15.2 Frequency diagrams, line graphs and scatter graphs

We are going to ...

- interpret and represent data in frequency diagrams, line graphs and scatter graphs

- plan and carry out investigations using data that includes measures

- predict the outcome of an investigation, look for patterns and check predictions.

We can use some graphs and charts to show if there is a link between two sets of data. For example, there might be a link between how tall someone is and how long their arms are.

frequency diagram
line graph
scatter graph

A class collected these sets of data about themselves. Which of these sets of data might have a link?

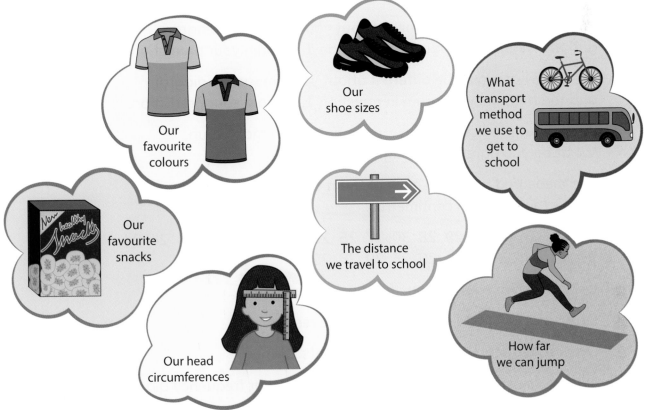

Our favourite colours

Our shoe sizes

What transport method we use to get to school

Our favourite snacks

The distance we travel to school

Our head circumferences

How far we can jump

Exercise 15.2

1   Halima measured the speed of vehicles passing her school for 30 minutes.
    This frequency diagram represents the data she collected.

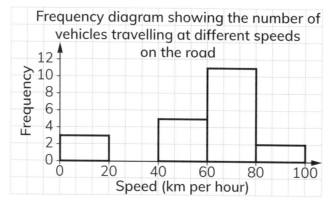

Tip

Remember, if the measurement is on the group boundary then it is recorded in the group above. For example, on this graph a vehicle traveling at 40 km per hour is put in the group 40 to 60 km per hour.

   a   How many vehicles were travelling 60 or more km per hour, but less than 80 km per hour?

   b   How many vehicles were travelling less than 60 km per hour?

   c   How many vehicles passed the school in total?

2   Imagine you represented the speed of vehicles passing your school for 30 minutes.

   a   Describe what equipment you would need and how you would collect the data.

   b   Predict what would be similar about your frequency diagram and the frequency diagram in question **1**. Explain your prediction.

   c   Predict what would be different about your frequency diagram and the frequency diagram in question **1**. Explain your prediction.

   d   Share your predictions with a partner or in a small group. What do you agree and disagree about?

3   A class measured how high each of them could jump vertically. These are the results in centimetres:

    25 31 33 18 28 36 29 28 30 27 25 29 32 19 28 24 24 24 24
    26 31 28 29 23 28 31 20 25 29 26 29.

   a   Decide on five equal groups for the measurements.

   b   Draw and complete a tally chart of the results.

   c   Draw a frequency diagram of the heights jumped.

   d   Write two sentences to describe the data in your frequency diagram.

4   Cheng left two thermometers in different places in the classroom.
He recorded the temperature on the thermometers every half an hour.
These line graphs show his results.

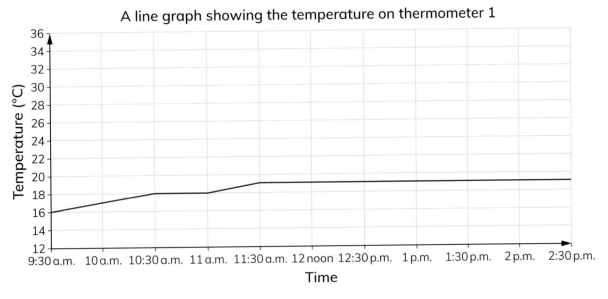

A line graph showing the temperature on thermometer 1

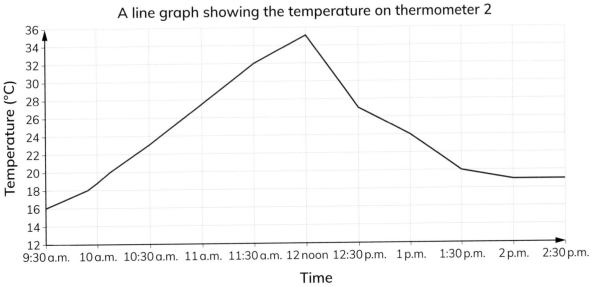

A line graph showing the temperature on thermometer 2

a   What was the temperature for thermometer 1 at 1 o'clock?

b   What was the time when thermometer 2 first showed 23°?

c   Use the line graphs to estimate the temperature on both
thermometers at 11:15 a.m.

d   Describe how the shape of the lines in the two graphs is different.

e   Suggest an explanation for the difference in the two graphs.

5   Dee measured her pulse rate every 10 minutes on a 1 hour run and for 20 minutes afterwards. These are her results:

Time	0	10	20	30	40	50	60	70	80
Pulse rate	66	102	102	118	106	130	130	88	68

Draw a line graph to represent the data in the table. Join the points on your graph with straight lines.

a   At what time was Dee's pulse rate 118 beats per minute?

b   What happened to Dee's pulse rate between 40 and 50 minutes?

c   Describe the pattern of the line in your graph.

d   Use your line graph to estimate Dee's pulse rate at:

   i   15 minutes   ii   35 minutes   iii   75 minutes

Worked example 2

A scatter graph is used to find out if there might be a relationship between two sets of data. If there is a relationship we can draw a line of best fit on the graph.

Draw a draw a line of best fit on the scatter graph.

A scatter graph showing the the heights of fathers and sons

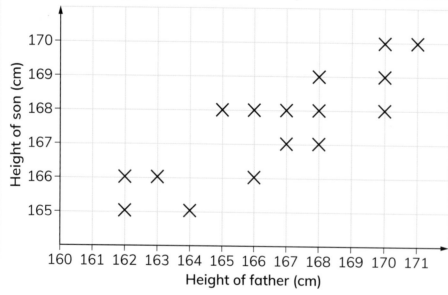

Continued

This slope is too steep. The points do not go up as quickly as this line.

The line needs to have the right slope.

This slope is not steep enough, the points go up quicker.

This slope is just right.

This line is too high.
Almost all the points are under it.

The line needs to go through the middle of the points so that there are just about the same number of points above the line as below the line.

This line is too low.
Almost all the points are above it.

This line is just right.

Continued

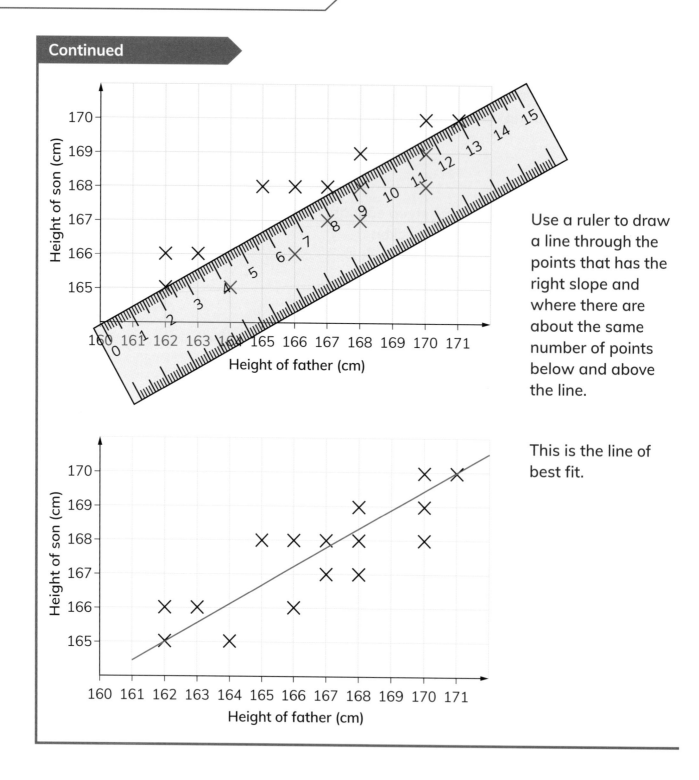

Use a ruler to draw a line through the points that has the right slope and where there are about the same number of points below and above the line.

This is the line of best fit.

6   Izzy has measured the hand spans and foot length of the children
    in her class and plotted them onto a scatter graph.
    The red line is her line of best fit.

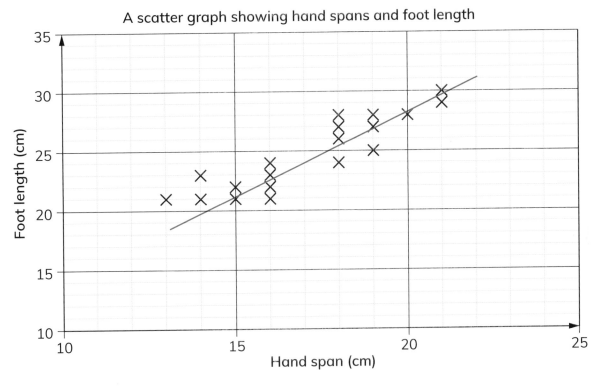

A scatter graph showing hand spans and foot length

a   What is the longest hand span in Izzy's class?

b   What is the shortest foot length in Izzy's class?

c   One child has a foot length of 26 cm, what is the measurement
    of their hand span?

d   A new child joins the class. Their hand span is 17 cm. Use the
    line of best fit to estimate the length of the new child's foot.

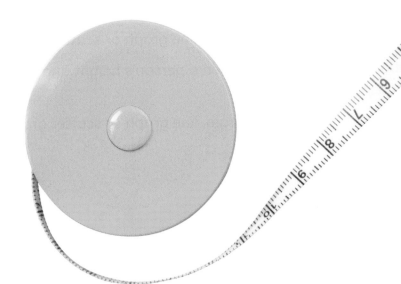

7 11 plants were grown. Each plant was measured and its number of leaves was counted. This table shows the data that was collected.

Height (cm)	6	11	15	8	12	17	15	18	9	11	13
Number of leaves	2	4	7	3	6	8	8	9	4	6	6

a Draw a scatter graph of the data in the table. Put the number of leaves along the vertical axis and the height on the horizontal axis.

b Does it look like there is a link between the height of the plants and the number of leaves? Describe the link.

The more leaves the plant has, the …

c Draw a line of best fit on the graph.

d Use your line of best fit to estimate how many leaves a plant might have if it was 14 cm tall.

e With your partner assess each of your lines of best fit. Are the lines:

- in the right direction

- not too steep

- steep enough

- not too high

- not too low.

8 Which graph would you use to represent the data in each of these investigations?

a Investigation: How quickly does hot water cool to room temperature?

Would you use a frequency diagram, line graph or a scatter graph?

b Investigation: What is the most common height for children in Stage 6?

Would you use a frequency diagram, line graph or scatter graph?

c Investigation: Is there a link between a person's height and how well they do in a science test?

Would you use a frequency diagram, line graph or scatter graph?

Think like a mathematician

Investigate your own problem where the data will be measured.
Ask your teacher to check your question before you start investigating.

You could choose one of these statistical questions to investigate.

- How does the temperature of water change in sunlight and in shade?

- Is there a link between head circumference and height?

- What is the most common distance that a person in our class can jump?

- Is there a link between how long a person's arm is and how far they can throw?

Discuss what question you will ask and who you will ask.

Write a sentence explaining what you think will be the result of your investigation and why.

Collect your data in a table.

Choose a way to represent your data. You could choose a frequency diagram, line graph or scatter graph. Explain why you chose that way of representing your data.

Describe any patterns you can see in your data.

Does your data suggest that your prediction was correct?

Use the information in your table, graph and diagrams to answer your statistical question.

Reflect on all the different ways that you can represent data.
Make a list of the different graphs, charts and diagrams you
have used. Include some that are not in this unit.

Look what I can do!

☐ I can interpret and represent data in frequency diagrams, line graphs and scatter graphs.

☐ I can plan and carry out investigations using data that includes measures.

☐ I can predict the outcome of an investigation, look for patterns and check predictions.

Check your progress

1 This pie chart shows the favourite types of films chosen by 20 people.

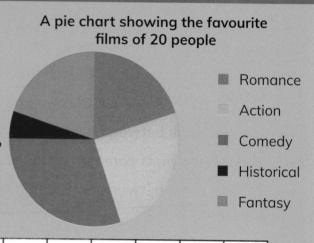

A pie chart showing the favourite films of 20 people

- Romance
- Action
- Comedy
- Historical
- Fantasy

a Which film type is most popular?

b Estimate what percentage of people chose fantasy films.

c How many people chose action films?

2 This table shows the temperature each day and the number of people who visited a garden.

Temperature (°C)	17	19	19	19	21	24	24	27	29
Number of visitors	14	15	18	16	24	28	24	28	26

Temperature (°C) cont.	27	25	22	16	16	15	14	14	12
Number of visitors cont.	30	30	20	12	15	7	5	10	6

a Plot the data from the table into a scatter graph.

b Draw a line of best fit.

c Use the line of best fit to predict how many visitors there would be if the temperature was 20 °C.

3 Describe how you would investigate how your pulse rate changes during and after exercise. Include:

- what equipment you would use

- how you would collect your data

- what you predict would happen

- which graph or chart you would use to represent your data and why.

16 ▶ The laws of arithmetic

Getting started

1   Mandisa calculates $7 \times 5 \times 8 \times 2$ mentally.

   She says, 'I can find the answer by multiplying 56 by 10.'

   Explain how she knows this.

2   Copy and complete this calculation.

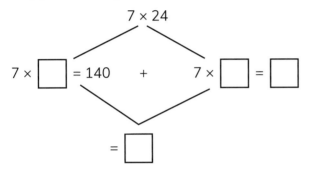

3   Calculate.

   a $14 + 12 \div 4$ b $17 - 6 \times 2$ c $8 \times 9 - 22$

4   Eva writes $6 + 9 \times 5 = 75$

   Is she correct? Explain your answer.

5   Copy the calculation and write in the missing numbers.

   a $3 \times \boxed{} + 9 = 30$ b $6 \times 8 - \boxed{} = 30$

Which is correct?

Can you remember the rules for calculations with different operations?

In Stage 5, you learned how the four operations, addition, subtraction, multiplication and division follow a particular order.

In this unit, you will learn how brackets can be used to change the order of operations.

〉 16.1 The laws of arithmetic

We are going to ...

- use the laws of arithmetic to simplify calculations

- understand the order of operations and use brackets to change the order of operations.

A rule tells you what you can and can't do.

In mathematics, you must follow the rule to do multiplication and division before addition and subtraction.

> associative law   brackets
> commutative law   distributive law
> order of operations

Arun and Marcus are calculating using the numbers 5, 6 and 7.

I want to multiply 6 and 7 and add my result to 5.

Arun writes $5 + 6 \times 7 = 47$

I want to add 5 and 6 and then multiply by 7.

How can Marcus write his calculation?

In this section, you will learn how to help Marcus write his calculation.

<table>
<tr><td colspan="2">Worked example 1</td></tr>
</table>

Why do these calculations give different answers?

A $3 \times 4 + 6$ B $3 \times (4 + 6)$

In calculation A we do the multiplication first:

$$3 \times 4 + 6 = 12 + 6$$
$$= 18$$

In calculation B we do the operation in brackets first:

$$3 \times (4 + 6) = 3 \times 10$$
$$= 30$$

The order of operations is:

Brackets

Multiplication and division

Addition and subtraction

The numbers and operations are the same, but the brackets identify the operation that is done first.

Answer: The calculations give different answers because the brackets in B change the order in which operations are done.

Exercise 16.1

1   Each learner is thinking of a number.

   Draw a diagram and write a calculation to show how to work out their numbers.

   a   Tariq is thinking of a number. He adds 7 to his number,
       then divides by 10. His answer is 1.

       What number is Tariq thinking of?

   b   Sonja is thinking of a number. She adds 5 to her number,
       then divides by 2. Her answer is 6.

       What number is Sonja thinking of?

   c   Pierre is thinking of a number. He multiplies his number by 3,
       then subtracts 2. His answer is 4.

       What number is Pierre thinking of?

   d   Lan is thinking of a number. She divides her number by 3,
       then adds 11. Her answer is 14.

       What number is Lan thinking of?

2   Calculate.

   a $(5 + 2) \times 3$ b $(3 \times 6) + 4$ c $3 \times (8 - 5)$

   d $(8 - 6) \times 4$ e $(3 + 7) \div 10$ f $(12 + 6) \div 3$

   One of the calculations gives the same answer even if the brackets
   are removed. Which calculation is it?

   Check your answers with your partner.

3   Are the following statements true or false? If a statement is false,
    write it out correctly.

   a $6 + 3 \times 4 = 18$ b $(6 + 3) \times 4 = 36$ c $(6 + 3) \times 4 = 18$

4   Put brackets in these calculations to make them correct.

   a $6 + 2 \times 5 = 40$ b $3 + 4 \times 2 + 4 = 42$

   c $3 \times 4 + 2 = 18$ d $4 + 3 + 2 \times 2 = 18$

> **Tip**
>
> You can draw a
> bracket round more
> than two numbers.

5   Use these numbers together with brackets and operation signs
    to make the target number.

    Example: 3, 4, 6   Target 42   Answer (3 + 4) × 6

    a   2, 5, 5   Target 35

    b   5, 7, 10   Target 20

    c   2, 5, 14   Target 18

> **Tip**
>
> Remember you can use the numbers in any order.

6   42 × 24 is equivalent to 42 × 2 × 12.

    Find three more ways to multiply 42 × 24.

    Write your answers in the form 42 × ☐ × ☐ .

    Choose one way to do the calculation.

    Explain to your partner why you chose this way.

7   Use the distributive law to calculate the following showing all the
    stages of your working.

    a   5 × (70 + 1)   b   6 × (60 − 3)

    c   7 × (90 + 2)   d   8 × (40 − 3)

8   Use the distributive law to work out these calculations.
    Show all your working.

    a   3 × 67   b   8 × 93

    c   7 × 48   d   9 × 79

9   Are the following statements true or false?
    Explain your decisions to your partner.

    a   8 + 5 − 7 = 8 + 7 − 5

    b   2 × (3 + 4) = 2 × 3 + 4

    c   10 × 5 ÷ 2 = 10 × (5 ÷ 2)

Look back at your work. Did you use the worked example to
help you? If you did, how did you use it?
Did you find it helpful to discuss your answers with your partner?
Did you make any improvements to your work after doing this?

Think like a mathematician

You have these cards:

| 1 | 2 | 3 | 4 | + | − | × | ÷ | (|) |

Use as many of the cards as you like to try to make the numbers from 11 to 20.

You are not allowed to make 2-digit numbers, for example, 12 + 3 is not allowed.

> **Tip**
>
> An example using all four numbers is:
> $(4 + 2) \times (3 − 1) = 12$

How many numbers can you make using all four number cards in the calculation?

You will show you are **specialising** when you find solutions to the problem.

Look what I can do!

☐ I can use the laws of arithmetic to simplify calculations.

☐ I understand the order of operations and use brackets to change the order of operations.

Check your progress

1 Write the missing number.

$10 \times 10 = \boxed{} \div (10 + 10)$

2 Calculate.

a $3 \times 4 + 6$ b $7 + 11 − 6$ c $14 \div 7 + 13$

d $(2 + 3) − (4 − 1)$ e $(14 − 6) \times (3 + 1)$ f $27 \div 9 \times 4$

3 Write the correct sign <, > or = to make each statement correct.

a $3 \times (4 + 5) \boxed{} 3 \times 4 + 5$ b $(8 + 6) \div 2 \boxed{} 8 + 6 \div 2$

4 Use these numbers together with brackets and operation signs to make the target number.

a 2, 3 and 4   Target 6   b 3, 4 and 7   Target 40

c 4, 12 and 15   Target 12   d 3, 5 and 18   Target 3

5 Put brackets in the calculation to make the answer 50.

$4 + 5 + 1 \times 5$

Getting started

1   The diagram shows three carrots on a coordinate grid.

There is a rabbit at the point (3, 2).

What are the coordinates of the carrot that is closest to the rabbit?

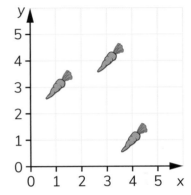

2   Write these coordinates in order of their distance from the x-axis. Start with the coordinate closest to the x-axis.

(0, 3)   (4, 5)   (5, 1)   (2, 2)

3   Describe the translation of the bottom triangle to the top triangle.

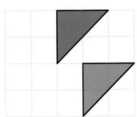

4   Copy this shape onto squared paper. Reflect the shape in the mirror lines shown to complete the pattern.

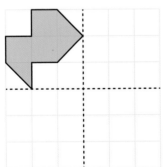

5   (2, 3), (5, 3) and (2, 6) are the coordinates of three vertices of a square. What are the coordinates of the other vertex?

Orienteering is a fun outdoor activity that is both a mental and physical challenge.

You are given a map, and you have to find your way to different check points that are located on the course.

The winner is the fastest person to find all the check points and finish the course.

You need to be able to read a map, so understanding coordinates is a very useful skill to have. You also need to be able to move from one point on the map to another, so understanding movement on a grid, and also turning through different angles is very useful. If you can run fast as well, you could be a winner!

> 17.1 Coordinates and translations

We are going to ...

- read and plot coordinates
- use knowledge of 2D shapes and coordinates to plot points to form lines and shapes
- translate 2D shapes on coordinate grids.

There are a lot of people, old and young, who love to play computer games. Some of the games are played on a coordinate grid and involve hitting exact points or moving shapes around.

Could you save the world if you were on a spaceship and there was an alien attack?

> axes   axis
> corresponding vertices
> translate

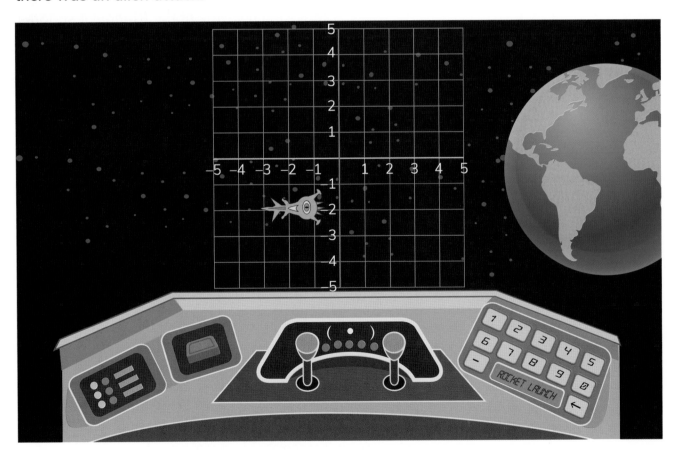

Worked example 1

Translate triangle ABC 4 squares left and
2 squares down. Label it triangle A′B′C′.
Write down the coordinates of the vertices A′, B′ and C′.

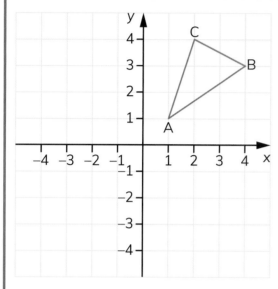

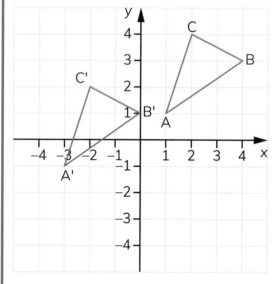

Move each vertex of the triangle 4 squares left and two squares down.

Vertex A on the original corresponds with vertex A′ (you say A dash) on the translated triangle. A and A′ are called corresponding vertices. B corresponds with B′ and C corresponds with C′.

Remember that when you write coordinates the x-axis number is first and the y-axis number is second. Coordinates can be positive or negative numbers, depending on where they are on the grid.

A′ (−3, −1)

B′ (0, 1)

C′ (−2, 2)

Exercise 17.1

1 Match each point on the grid to its correct coordinates.
One is done for you: **A** and **ii**.

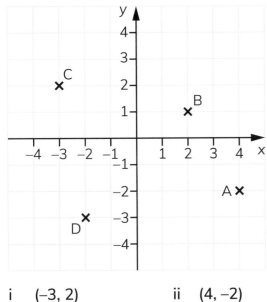

Tip

$(+, +) \rightarrow$ (right, up)
$(+, -) \rightarrow$ (right, down)
$(-, +) \rightarrow$ (left, up)
$(-, -) \rightarrow$ (left, down)

i   (−3, 2)   ii   (4, −2)   iii   (−2, −3)   iv   (2, 1)

2 Here is a treasure map.

Write down the coordinates of:

a   the volcano

b   the treasure chest

c   the shark

d   the pirate ship.

3   Draw axes from −5 to +5 on squared paper.
    Draw a trapezium with vertices at P (−2, 1),
    Q (−1, 3), R (2, 3) and S (3, 1).

> **Tip**
>
> For P′ you say P dash.
> For P″ you say
> P double dash.

    a Translate trapezium PQRS 2 squares right
    and 1 square up. Label the trapezium
    P′Q′R′S′ and write down the coordinates
    of its vertices.

    b Translate trapezium PQRS 2 squares left
    and 5 square down. Label the trapezium P″Q″R″S″
    and write down the coordinates of its vertices.

Think like a mathematician 1

The diagram shows points A, B and C on a coordinate grid.

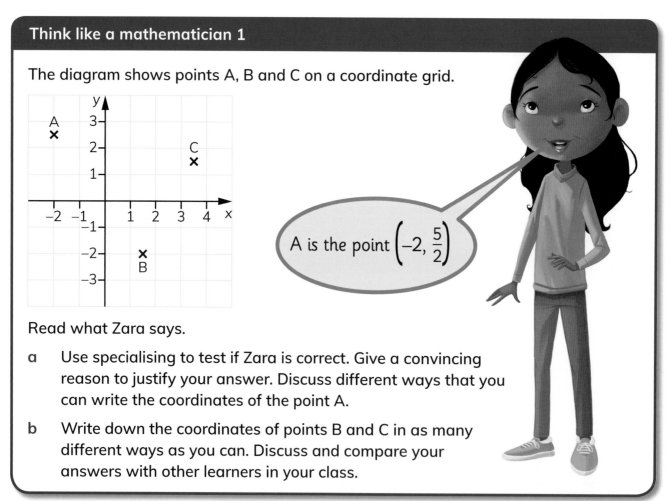

A is the point $\left(-2, \dfrac{5}{2}\right)$

Read what Zara says.

a   Use specialising to test if Zara is correct. Give a convincing
    reason to justify your answer. Discuss different ways that you
    can write the coordinates of the point A.

b   Write down the coordinates of points B and C in as many
    different ways as you can. Discuss and compare your
    answers with other learners in your class.

4 Draw axes from –6 to +6 on squared paper.
Plot the points J (–2, 2), K (–2, –1) and L (1, –1).

a Write down the coordinates of M so that J, K, L and M are the vertices of a square.

b Write down two possible coordinates of M so that M is a point on the line segment JL.

c Write down two possible coordinates of M so that J, K, L and M are the vertices of a parallelogram.

d Write down two possible coordinates of M so that J, K, L and M are the vertices of a kite.

e In which parts **a** to **d** are there more than two answers for the coordinates of M? Give a convincing reason to justify why by generalising.

> **Tip**
>
> Remember that coordinates do not always have to be whole numbers. You can use fractions and decimals too.

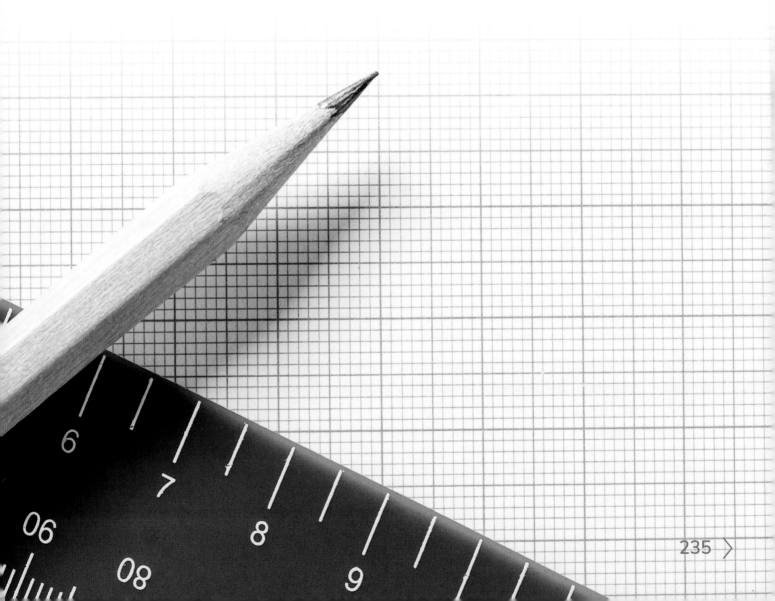

Think like a mathematician 2

The diagram shows triangles A to I.

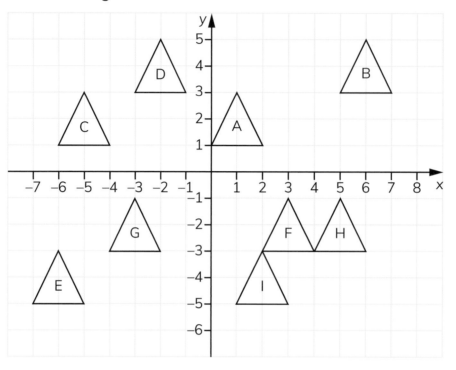

Here are nine translation cards.

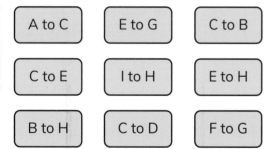

a   Classify the cards into groups of equivalent translations.
    Describe the translation for each group.

b   Write two more translation cards, using four of the triangles A
    to I, that could make a different group. Describe the translation
    for this group.

Think like a mathematician 3

Lukman is making a pattern by translating a kite. He uses the same translation every time. The diagram shows the 1st and 2nd kites.

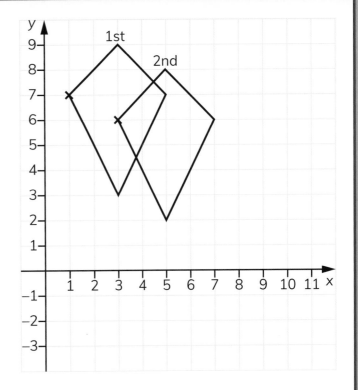

a   What translation does he use?

b   Copy the diagram and draw the 3rd and 4th kites in the pattern.

c   Lukman marks a cross on the same vertex of the kite every time he translates the kite. Copy and complete this table showing the coordinates of this vertex.

Kite	1st	2nd	3rd	4th
Coordinates	(1, 7)	(3, 6)		

d   Make a conjecture about the x-coordinate as the pattern continues.

e   Make a conjecture about the y-coordinate as the pattern continues.

f   Without drawing the 5th and 6th kites in the pattern, write down the coordinates of the vertex marked with a cross for each kite. Give a convincing reason to justify your answer.

g   Draw your own pattern on a coordinate grid using your own shape and translation. Investigate what happens to the coordinates of one vertex of your shape as the pattern continues.

h   Discuss your patterns and answers with other learners in your class.

In this section you have:
1   Used coordinates with positive and negative numbers.
2   Used coordinates with decimals, fractions and whole numbers.
3   Used your knowledge of 2D shapes on a coordinate grid.
4   Translated shapes on a coordinate grid.

a   Which of these four skills have you found
     i   the easiest   ii   the hardest?
b   What can you do to improve the skill which you found
     the hardest?

Look what I can do!

☐   I can read and plot coordinates.

☐   I can use knowledge of 2D shapes and coordinates to plot points
     to form lines and shapes.

☐   I can translate 2D shapes on coordinate grids.

> 17.2 Reflections

We are going to ...

• reflect 2D shapes in horizontal, vertical and diagonal mirror lines.

What do you see when you look in a mirror? You see a
reflection of yourself and the world around you. Artists use
reflections in their paintings. Even the very earliest artists
noticed that shiny objects or water or even a person's eyes showed
a reflection, and they tried to include these in their artworks to make
them as realistic as possible.

diagonal mirror line

When you next draw a picture, try to include a reflection, but remember that as a piece of art, it doesn't have to be a true reflection ...

Worked example 2

Reflect this trapezium in the diagonal mirror line.

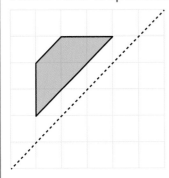

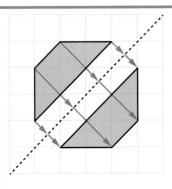

Take one vertex of the trapezium at a time.
Draw arrows (red) to the mirror line,
then draw the same length arrows (blue)
the other side of the mirror line.
Join the vertices with straight lines to
complete the reflected trapezium.

Exercise 17.2

 1   Which drawings show correct reflections of triangle A?

a 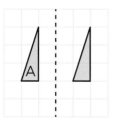   b 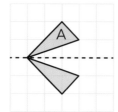   c 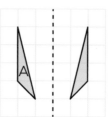   d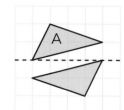

2   Copy each diagram and reflect the shape in the horizontal and vertical mirror lines.

a 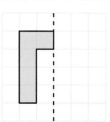   b 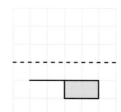   c 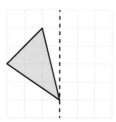   d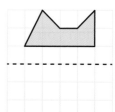

Think like a mathematician 1

This is part of Arun's homework.

Question: Reflect shape A in the diagonal line
of symmetry.

Label your answer shape B.

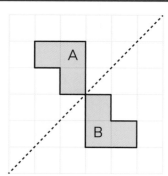

This is the method that Arun uses.

I use tracing paper to trace shape A and the mirror line. Then I turn my tracing paper round until the mirror line on my tracing paper fits over the mirror line on the diagram. I can then see where shape B is, so I can draw it in on the diagram.

a   Has Arun drawn shape B correctly? Explain your answer.

b   Critique Arun's method. Is it correct? If it isn't correct, how can you improve it so it is correct?

c   Discuss your answers to parts **a** and **b** with other learners in your class.

3 Copy each diagram and reflect the shape in the diagonal mirror lines.
The first one has been started for you.

a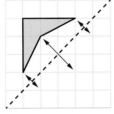

b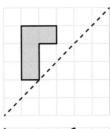

c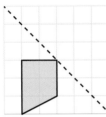

d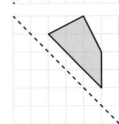

Tip

Use tracing paper or a mirror to help you.

4 a Describe the characteristics of the mirror line for each of these reflections.

i

ii

iii

Tip

Is the mirror line horizontal, vertical or diagonal?

b Copy each diagram in part **a** and draw in the correct mirror line for each reflection.

Think like a mathematician 2

Work with a partner for this activity.

On a piece of squared paper, make a copy of this grid and mirror line.

In the shaded region draw a quadrilateral. Swap pieces of paper with a partner. Reflect their quadrilateral in the mirror line. Swap back the pieces of paper and mark each other's work. Discuss any mistakes that have been made.

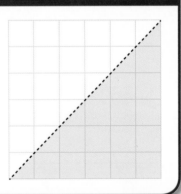

Look what I can do!

☐ I can reflect 2D shapes in horizontal, vertical and diagonal mirror lines.

> 17.3 Rotations

We are going to ...

- rotate 2D shapes 90 ° around a vertex.

When you go to a play park, have you ever looked at the floor? Many play parks now have rubber flooring, which is good in all weathers and it doesn't hurt very much if you fall over! Have you ever thought about who designs the flooring, and how they do it? This is where knowing how to turn, reflect and translate shapes comes in really useful. Have a look at the flooring in this picture. Can you see any shapes that have been turned, reflected or translated?

anticlockwise
centre of rotation
clockwise
corresponding vertices
rotate

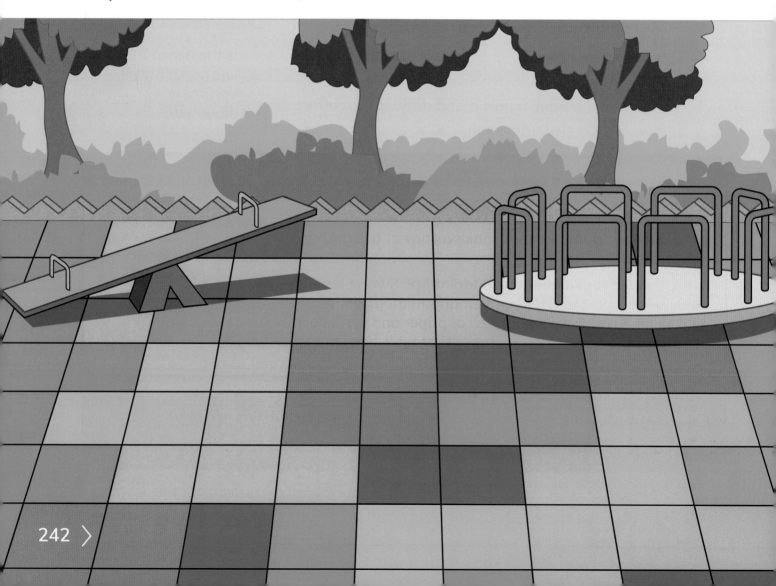

Worked example 3

Rotate triangle A 90° clockwise about the centre of rotation marked C. Label your answer triangle B.

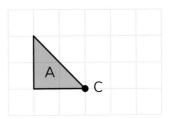

Step 1

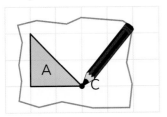

Trace the shape, then put the point of your pencil on the centre of rotation.

Step 2

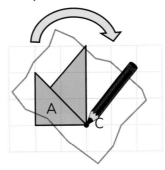

Start turning the tracing paper 90° (a quarter turn) clockwise. Make sure you keep the pencil on top of the tracing paper as the centre of rotation.

Step 3

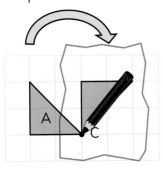

Once the turn is completed make a note of where the new triangle is.

Step 4

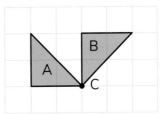

Draw the new triangle onto the grid and label it B.

Exercise 17.3

1 Copy each diagram and rotate the shapes 90 ° clockwise about the
   centre of rotation C.

   a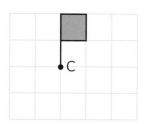

   b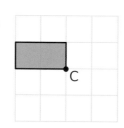

Think like a mathematician 1

This is part of Sita's homework.

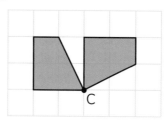

Question: Rotate shape A 90° anticlockwise about
centre C. Label your shape B.

Sita has correctly rotated the shape but has forgotten to
label the shapes A and B.

a Which is shape A and which is shape B? Explain how you know.

b Describe the difference between a 90 ° rotation clockwise and
     a 90 ° rotation anticlockwise.

c Discuss your answers to parts **a** and **b** with other learners in
     your class. Also discuss ways to remember which way is clockwise
     and which way is anticlockwise.

Tip

Clockwise: Anticlockwise:

2   Copy each diagram and rotate the shapes 90° anticlockwise about
    the centre of rotation C.

a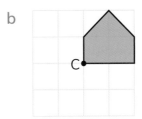

b

3   The diagrams **i** to **vi** all show shape A rotated to shape B.
    The centre of rotation is shown by a dot (•).

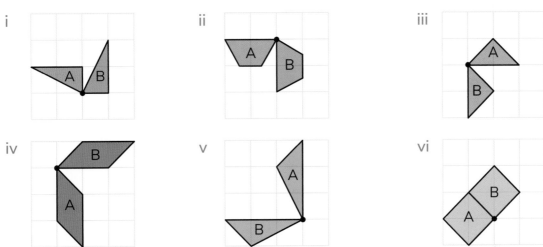

a   Sort the diagrams into two groups.
    Describe the characteristics of each group.

b   Compare and discuss your answers with other learners in your class.
    Did you all choose the same groups or did some of you have
    different groups?

Think like a mathematician 2

Hamila draws a triangle on a grid.
She translates it 3 squares right and 2 squares down.
She joins the corresponding vertices with straight lines.
This is what her diagram looks like.

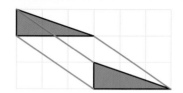

Tip

Corresponding vertices are vertices that are in the same position on the shape before and after a transformation.

a   Copy this diagram.
Reflect the triangle in the mirror line.
Join the corresponding vertices with straight lines.

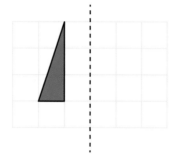

b   Copy this diagram.

Rotate the triangle 90° clockwise about centre C.
Join the corresponding vertices with straight lines.

c   Make a conjecture about the lines that join the corresponding vertices of the triangles after a

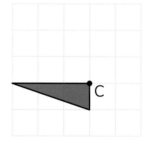

i   translation   ii   reflection   iii   rotation?

d   Discuss your answers to part **c** with other learners in your class. Decide which word is missing from this general rule:

When you translate or reflect a triangle, the lines joining the corresponding vertices will always be _____ , but when you rotate a triangle the lines joining the corresponding vertices will never be _____ .

e   Does the general rule in part **d** only work for triangles, or does it work for any 2D shape? Explain why you think this is the case.

4   Copy each diagram and rotate the shapes 90° about the centre of
    rotation C, using the direction shown.

a   clockwise

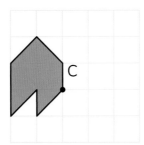

b   anticlockwise

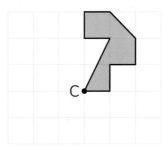

Here are some words and phrases that you have
used in this section.

Rotation   Anticlockwise   Centre of rotation

        Corresponding vertices   Clockwise

Take it in turns with a partner to choose one of the words or
phrases above.
Explain the meaning of the word or phrase to your partner.
a   Did you understand each other's explanations?
b   Are there any words that you are not sure about? If there are,
    find out what they mean and make sure you understand them.

Look what I can do!

☐   I can rotate 2D shapes 90° around a vertex.

Check your progress

1   The diagram shows points A, B, C and D on a coordinate grid.

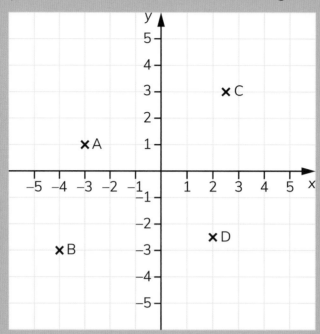

Write down the coordinates of
a   A   b   B   c   C   d   D

2   Draw axes from –6 to +6 on squared paper.

Plot the points E (–1, 1), F (–1, –2) and G (4, 1).

a   Write down the coordinates of H so that E, F, G and H are the vertices of a rectangle.

b   Write down two possible coordinates of H so that H is a point on the line segment EF.

c   Write down two possible coordinates of H so that E, F, G and H are the vertices of a parallelogram.

Continued

3 Copy this diagram. Translate the trapezium 5 squares left and 4 squares up.

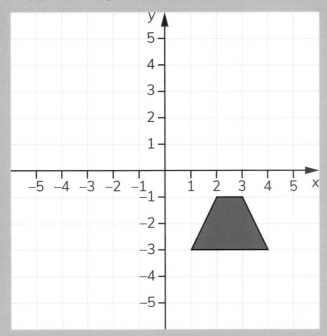

4 Copy the diagram and reflect the shape in the diagonal mirror line.

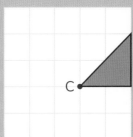

5 Copy each diagram and rotate the shapes 90° about the centre of rotation C, using the direction shown.

a   clockwise

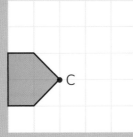

b   anticlockwise

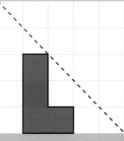

> Project 6

Considering coordinates

Arun is investigating the coordinates of the corners of squares drawn on a grid.

He starts by drawing this square:

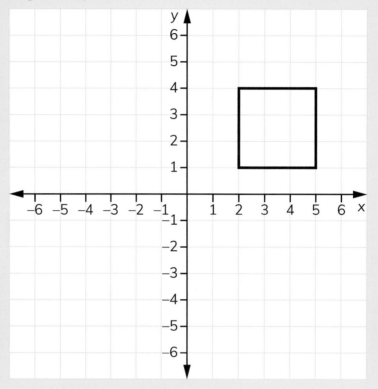

He finds the coordinates of the corners of the square and looks for patterns in these coordinates.

What patterns do you notice? Can you explain why this is happening?

Continued

Arun draws some more squares.

I think that when you draw a square on a coordinate grid, if you choose one corner then it will have the same x-coordinate as one of the other corners. It isn't possible to draw a square where all the corners have different x-coordinates.

Do you agree or disagree with Arun? Can you draw a square on a coordinate grid where all the corners have different x-coordinates?

Arun is reflecting squares in a mirror line.
He draws this dotted mirror line to reflect his square:

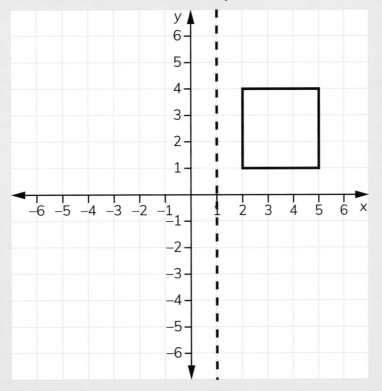

Arun reflects the square in the mirror line and then finds the coordinates of the corners of the new square.
He looks for patterns in these coordinates.

Continued

What patterns do you notice? Can you explain why this is happening?

Arun draws some more squares and mirror lines.

I think that when you reflect a square in a mirror line, if you choose one corner of the new square then it will have the same x-coordinate or y-coordinate as one corner of the old square. It isn't possible to reflect a square where all the corners of the reflected square have completely different coordinates to the corners of the original square.

Do you agree or disagree with Arun? Can you draw a square and a mirror line on a coordinate grid where all the corners of the reflected square have different x-coordinates and y-coordinates compared to the corners of the original square?

Glossary

anticlockwise	turning in the opposite direction to the hands of a clock	242
area	the size a surface covers. It is measured in square units, such as square metres (m^2) and square centimetres (cm^2).	100
associative law	when more than two numbers are added or multiplied, you can do the calculations in any order. For example:	

$$8 + 3 + 4 = 8 + 3 + 4 \qquad 5 \times 2 \times 3 = 5 \times 2 \times 3$$

$$11 + 4 = 8 + 7 \qquad\qquad 10 \times 3 = 5 \times 6$$

$$15 = 15 \qquad\qquad\qquad 30 = 30 \qquad\qquad 224$$

average	a measure used to find the middle or most typical value in a set of data	39
axes	plural of axis	231
axis	a number line drawn on a coordinate grid and labelled either x or y. The x-axis is horizontal and the y-axis is vertical.	231
bar chart	a graph representing data using bars so that quantities and number can be easily compared	205
bimodal	a set of data that has two modes	39
bisect	cut exactly in half	65
brackets	a pair of symbols ( ) used to enclose sections of a mathematical expression. For example:	

$2 + 7$ is a mathematical expression

$$4 \times (2 + 7) = 4 \times 9 = 36$$

a pair of symbols

The part in the brackets is calculated first. 224

decimal number	a number written in decimal notation, for example 34.518	115, 196
decimal place	the position of a digit to the right of the decimal point in a decimal number, the number 45.674 has three decimal places	115, 196
decimal point	the decimal point separates whole numbers from decimal places	

10	1	0.1	0.01	0.001
5	7	0	8	2

you read 57.082 as 'fifty-seven point zero eight two' — 12, 196

decompose	break down a number into its parts (hundreds, tens and ones). For example, 456 is 400 + 50 + 6.	12
denominator	the bottom number of a fraction. It tells you how many equal parts a shape or quantity has been divided into. For example, in $\frac{1}{3}$ the denominator is 3.	86, 118, 192
diagonal	line that joins opposite vertices (corners) of a quadrilateral, a pentagon, a hexagon, etc.	65
diagonal mirror line	a mirror line which is not horizontal or vertical	238
diameter	line joining two points on the circumference that goes through the centre of the circle	72
digit	a symbol used to write a number. The decimal system uses ten digits: 0, 1, 2, 3, 4, 5, 6, 7, 8, 9	12
direct proportion	direct proportion is the relationship between two variables whose ratio remains constant. As the first variable increases (decreases) the second variable increases (decreases) for example, if you buy more apples you pay more money.	169

distributive law	when two numbers are multiplied, you can break the multiplication fact into a sum of two other multiplication facts. For example: 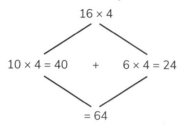	224
dividend	the number being divided. For example: 31 ÷ 3 = 10 r1 ↑ dividend	139, 200
divisible	can be divided without a remainder. For example, 108 is divisible by 3.	143
divisor	a number by which another number is divided, for example: 30 ÷ 3 = 10 ↑ divisor	139, 200
dot plot	a graph representing data using a dot to show the frequency of each number or category	205
divisibility test	a test for finding whether one whole number is divisible by another. For example, a number can be divided by 4 if the number made by the last two digits (tens and ones) is divisible by 4, and divisible by 8 if the number made by the last three digits (hundreds, tens and ones) is divisible by 8.	143
equally likely outcomes	outcomes with the same probability as each other	124
equilateral triangle	a triangle in which all the sides are equal in length and so all the angles are equal in size	184
equivalent fractions	fractions that are equal in value. For example, $\frac{2}{4}$ and $\frac{1}{2}$ are equivalent.	93

equivalent ratio	equivalent ratios are equal in value. For example, 1 : 2 is equivalent to 2 : 4 and 4 : 8. They are formed by multiplying or dividing their terms by the same number, for example:	

$$\times 2 \left\{ \begin{array}{l} 1 : 2 \\ 2 : 4 \\ 4 : 8 \end{array} \right\} \times 2 \qquad \div 2 \left\{ \begin{array}{l} 4 : 8 \\ 2 : 4 \\ 1 : 2 \end{array} \right\} \div 2$$

166

event	a set of some possible outcomes. An event can have one outcome or more than one outcome.	124
factor	a whole number that divides exactly into another number. For example, 2 × 3 = 6 so 2 and 3 are factors of 6.	30, 143
frequency diagram	a graph that shows groups of data in vertical bars	213
hundredth	one part in one hundred equal parts. As a decimal it is written as 0.01.	12
improper fraction	a fraction greater than or equal to one whole. The numerator is greater than or equal to the denominator. For example, $\frac{5}{3}$ (five-thirds).	86
integer	a positive or negative number or zero but not a decimal or fraction	51
isosceles triangle	a triangle in which two sides are equal in length and so the opposite two angles are equal in size	184
justify	give a reason	65
line graph	a graph joining data points with a line. It often shows changes over time.	213
mean	the average of a set of data, calculated by adding up all the values and dividing by the number of values	39
median	the middle value in an ordered set of data	39
mixed number	a whole number and a proper fraction combined. For example, $1\frac{3}{4}$.	86
mode	the value that occurs most often in a set of data	39
multiple	the result of multiplying a number by a positive whole number.	30, 143

mutually exclusive events	events that cannot happen at the same time, for example, it is not possible to roll a '5' and roll a '2' on the same dice at the same time	124
nearest	closest to	16
negative number	a number that is less than zero. We use a – sign to show a negative number.	

$$-10 \qquad 0 \qquad 10$$
$$\longleftarrow \quad \text{negative numbers} \mid \text{positive numbers} \quad \longrightarrow$$

51

numerator	the top number of a fraction. It tells you how many parts you have.	86, 192
operator	you can use a fraction as an operator to find a fraction of an amount. For example, to find $\frac{3}{4}$ of something, you either divide by 4 and then multiply by 3 or multiply by 3 and then divide by 4.	86, 89, 192
order	(of rotational symmetry) is the number of times the shape looks the same in one full turn	78
order of operations	the order in which mathematical operations should be done: • brackets • multiplication and division • addition and subtraction	224
outcome	the result of one trial in a probability experiment	124
parallel	lines that do not meet, they always stay the same distance apart	65
per cent	the number of parts out of every hundred	89
percentage	the number of parts out of a hundred. The symbol is %.	89
pie chart	a chart representing data using a divided circle where each section represents part of the total in proportion to other categories	205

place value	the value of a digit determined by its position. For example, in 830.467 the 7 has a value of 7 thousandths (0.007).	

100	10	1	•	0.1	0.01	0.001
8	3	0	•	4	6	7

12

position-to-term rule	the rule that defines the value of each term with respect to its position. For example, for the sequence 6, 12, 18, 24, ... the position-to-term rule is position number times 6.

Position	Term
1	6
2	12
3	18
4	24

22

positive number	a number that is greater than zero

negative numbers | positive numbers

51

prism	a 3D shape with two parallel identical faces. All the other faces are rectangles.	149
probability	the chance that a particular outcome will occur, measured as a ratio of the total of possible outcomes	124
probability experiment	a situation where a number of trials are carried out to explore the probability of something happening	124
product	the answer when two or more numbers are multiplied together. For example, the product of 3 and 5 is 15 because $3 \times 5 = 15$	135, 196
proper fraction	a fraction smaller than one whole. The numerator is smaller than the denominator. For example, $\frac{2}{5}$.	86, 192

scatter graph	a graph used for 2 sets of data to see if there is a relationship between them	213
simplest form	a fraction where the numerator and denominator cannot be reduced any further to give an equivalent fraction. For example, $\frac{1}{2}$ is the simplest form of $\frac{6}{12}$.	93, 166

simplest form (ratio)   a ratio where the terms cannot be reduced any further by dividing them by the same number. For example, 4 : 5 is the simplest form of 16 : 20.

$\div2 \begin{cases} 16 : 20 \\ 8 : 10 \\ 4 : 5 \end{cases} \div2$ 166

simplify a fraction   reduce the numerator and denominator of a fraction to smaller numbers. This can be done in a series of steps, for example:

$\frac{4}{8} \xrightarrow{\div2} \frac{2}{4} \xrightarrow{\div2} \frac{1}{2}$ 93

square number   a number you get when you multiply an integer by itself. For example, 16 is a square number.

$4 \times 4 = 4^2 = 16$ 27

surface area	the total area of the faces of a 3D shape	149
tenth	one part in ten equal parts. As a decimal it is written as 0.1.	12
term	part of a sequence separated by commas. For example, in the sequence 6, 12, 18, 24, ... the second term is 12.	22
term-to-term rule	a rule you can use to find the next number in the sequence. For example, in the sequence 6, 12, 18, 24, ... the term-to-term rule is 'add 6 to the previous term'.	22

thousandth	one part in one thousand equal parts. As a decimal it is written as 0.001.	12
translate	to move a shape a number of units left or right and up or down	231
trapezia	plural of trapezium	65
unit fraction	a fraction with a numerator of 1, for example $\frac{1}{2}$ or $\frac{1}{5}$	192
variable	a quantity that can change to take on different values. A variable can be represented by any letter of the alphabet.	56
Venn diagram	a diagram using hoops to sort items such as objects, shapes or numbers. It can show the relationship between sets of items.	143
volume	the amount of space taken up by an object, liquid or gas	155
waffle diagram	a diagram representing data using a divided rectangle where each section represents part of the total in proportion to the other categories	205

Acknowledgements

It takes a number of people to put together a new series of resources and their comments, support and encouragement have been really important to us.

From Mary Wood: With thanks to Katherine Bird, my editor, for her wise words, to my son, David, for his willingness to talk mathematics and respond to my IT needs and to my husband, Norman, for being there when it was tough going.

From Emma Low: With thanks to Katherine and Caroline for their indispensable ideas and feedback, and also to Andy and our daughters Natasha, Jessica and Phoebe for their love and support and occasional very helpful puzzle and problem testing.

From Cambridge University Press: We would like to thank the following people: Katherine Bird and Suzanne Thurston for their support for the authors; Lynne McClure for her feedback and comments on early sections of the manuscript; Thomas Carter, Caroline Walton, Laura Collins, Charlotte Griggs, Gabby Martin, Elizabeth Scurfield, Berenice Howard-Smith, Zohir Naciri, Emma McCrea and Eddie Rippeth as part of the team at Cambridge preparing the resources. We would also like to particularly thank all of the anonymous reviewers for their time and comments on the manuscript and as part of the endorsement process.

The authors and publishers acknowledge the following sources of copyright material and are grateful for the permissions granted. While every effort has been made, it has not always been possible to identify the sources of all the material used, or to trace all copyright holders. If any omissions are brought to our notice, we will be happy to include the appropriate acknowledgements on reprinting.

Thanks to the following for permission to reproduce images:

Cover Photo: Omar Aranda (Beehive Illustration)

Siriporn Kaenseeya / EyeEm/GI; Maria Nuzzo / EyeEm/GI; brizmaker/GI; lucadp/GI; simonkr/GI; Robert Briggs/GI; Isabel Pavia/GI; Alexander Hassenstein/GI; Difydave/GI; Roc Canals/GI; Aitor Diago/GI; Jan Hakan Dahlstrom/GI; Richard Drury/GI; Teo Lannie/GI; Satakorn Sukontakajonkul / EyeEm/GI; fhm/GI; Jennifer A Smith/GI; photography by Torsten Spiller/GI; Jurgita Vaicikeviciene / EyeEm/GI; Carol Yepes/GI; Tahreer Photography/GI; Tom Werner/GI; BanksPhotos/GI; John Keeble/GI; Yulia-Images/GI; © Jackie Bale/GI; Westend61/GI; Welcome to buy my photos/GI; Rachel Husband/GI; Peter Dazeley/GI; AlpamayoPhoto/GI; Science Photo Library/GI; Vicki Jauron, Babylon and Beyond Photography/GI; Richard Drury/GI; Michael Burrell/GI; alf255/GI; blackred/GI; Vadim Dorofeev/GI; inbj/GI; alexsl/GI; duncan1890/GI; Massimo Ravera/GI; Peter Dazeley/GI; mr_morton/GI; aryos/GI; Daniela Pelazza / EyeEm/GI; urbancow/GI; Mark Dadswell/GI; Richard Drury/GI; Fabian Plock / EyeEm/GI; Don Farrall/GI; Roberto Sorin Opreanu / EyeEm/ GI; shomos uddin/GI; Morsa Images/GI; powerofforever/GI; Thomas Barwick/GI; Luis Alvarez/GI; kahramaninsan/GI; Flickr; stockcam/GI; HUIZENG HU/GI; alvarez/GI; Boris SV/GI; Fotosearch/GI; Arx0nt/GI; alvarez/GI; sturti/GI; Sergio Amiti/GI; owngarden/GI; chang/GI; Riou/GI; Dougal Waters/GI; gldburger/GI; JLGutierrez/GI; Westend61/GI; © Philippe LEJEANVRE/GI; Jasmin Merdan/GI; Eugen Wais / EyeEm/GI; Bob Ell / EyeEm/GI; Westend61/GI; Andriy Onufriyenko/GI; Klaus Vedfelt/GI; Lilly Roadstones/GI; Jamie Grill/GI; Christiane Jähnel / EyeEm/GI; Vlatko Gasparic/GI; Sanga Park / EyeEm/GI; Jacky Parker Photography/GI; EDUARD MUZHEVSKYI / SCIENCE PHOTO LIBRARY/GI; Tom Werner/GI; Tom Werner/GI; malerapaso/GI; Pachai Leknettip / EyeEm/GI; Matteo Colombo/GI; Catherine Falls Commercial/GI; Catherine Falls Commercial/GI; Zocha_K/GI; zodebala/GI; MirageC/GI; Adam Gault/GI; Andrew Brookes/GI.

GI = Getty Images